Business Mathematics

INSTRUCTOR'S MANUAL

J. Roland Kelley Tarrant County Junior College

Jimmy C. McKenzie Tarrant County Junior College

Alton W. Evans Tarrant County Junior College

Houghton Mifflin Company • **Boston**

Dallas • Geneva, Illinois • Hopewell, New Jersey • Palo Alto • London

Printed in the U.S.A.

ISBN: 0-395-30671-X

TABLE OF CONTENTS

TO THE INSTRUCTOR

Business Mathematics is designed to provide the mathematical background that your students will need (1) in other business courses, (2) in their careers in business, and (3) in their roles as informed consumers. Early chapters provide the student with an opportunity to review basic mathematics. The remaining chapters acquaint the student with the mathematics of key areas of business activity, including data processing, marketing, accounting, finance, insurance, real estate, transportation, and consumerism.

The amount of classroom time often differs from college to college or even within the same college. Student ability also varies from group to group. Thus, one of the key considerations in the selection of topics was our desire to develop a flexible text that can be adapted to individual class needs. The material is divided into learning units that develop a single concept (or several closely related concepts). This will enable you to select the concepts that you believe are most appropriate and to present them in a sequence that reflects your own particular teaching objectives.

Arrangement of Materials

The material has been arranged in five major parts. Each part is divided into chapters containing two or more learning units.

Student performance objectives precede each chapter, providing the students with a handy study guide. At the end of each chapter is a series of problems under the heading of Self-Evaluation. These problems are included to enable students to check their comprehension of the material covered in the chapter. Answers to the self-evaluation problems are included as an appendix in the student text.

The organization of a learning unit consists of (1) explanations of where, why, and how each concept is used in business, (2) examples illustrating application of the concepts and of problem-solving techniques, and (3) realistic exercise problems of graduated difficulty that enable students to apply the concepts to typical business situations. These exercise problems include a variety of word and computational problems that provide valuable training for actual business situations. Business forms have been included in the problems, when appropriate, to help students become familiar with the type of forms commonly used in business.

Student Evaluation

Answers to the odd-number problems are included as an appendix in the student

text. Enabling the students to receive immediate feedback while working the odd-numbered problems should help develop their self-confidence.
Answers to even-numbered problems are included in the instructor's edition.
You may wish to make these answers available to the students or use some of
the even-numbered problems for quizzes or tests.

Problems for self-evaluation are provided at the end of each chapter.
After completing the chapter, students should complete the self-evaluation
section and check their answers against the answer key. Students who have
difficulty with these problems should be encouraged to restudy the concepts
and problem-solving techniques explained in the chapter.

Aids for the Instructor

A test bank is included in this instructor's edition that will enable you
to pretest and post-test all of the concepts covered in the text. You may
wish to pretest at the beginning of or during each part. This will help
you to determine the areas to emphasize in your explanation or review of
the material. Pretesting will enable you to prescribe the material the student needs to study or restudy. The test bank questions are identified by
learning unit. This will make it possible for you to post-test as often as
necessary and will save your time in preparing the tests. The test bank
will enable you to tailor your tests to match the needs of individual student groups.

Transparency masters are provided to help you illustrate some of the
key concepts presented in this text. In addition to the answers, solutions
are provided for those problems that may require analysis or whose solutions
are lengthy.

Chapter 1

Whole Numbers and Decimal Numbers

A.   Purpose

The ability to perform the fundamental operations of arithmetic (add, subtract, multiply, divide) with reasonable skill is essential to success in
many business courses and occupations. Many students who enroll for a
course in business mathematics need a review of basic mathematics before be-
ing able to apply these skills to the solution of business problems. This
chapter provides the student an opportunity to review the fundamental operations of arithmetic involving whole numbers and decimal numbers.

B.   Comments

Following a discussion of the material in the learning units in Chapter 1,
the instructor may assign the odd-numbered problems and have the students
check their answers in the answer key. This will provide an opportunity
for the instructor to circulate through the classroom and help any students
who experience difficulty with the fundamental operations covered in this
chapter.

C.   Solutions

Learning Unit 1.1

Reading and Writing Numbers

1. eighteen
2. three hundred seventy
3. four thousand, seventy-three

4. sixty-two thousand, one hundred fifty-two
5. one hundred seventy thousand, six hundred
6. one million, four hundred twenty thousand
7. thirty-nine million, forty thousand, three hundred twenty-seven
8. one billion, seventy million, six hundred thousand
9. three hundredths
10. seven hundred sixty-five thousandths
11. one hundred twenty-two and five tenths
12. seventy-six and eighty-two hundredths
13. nine and three hundred sixty-three hundred-thousandths
14. one hundred forty-six and one thousandth
15. five and two hundred sixty-three millionths
16. one thousand and nine thousand three ten-thousandths
17. 825
18. 4,010,009
19. 7,200
20. 201,030,000
21. 48,203
22. 706,000
23. 123.456
24. 9,003.0006
25. 401.00034
26. 15.000314
27. 13,240.065
28. 42.19
29. 3;7;thirty-seven hundredths
30. 1;0;6;one and six hundredths
31. 4;6;0;3;8;forty-six and thirty-eight thousandths
32. 1;4;6;9;2;6;1;one hundred forty-six and nine thousand two hundred
    sixty-one thousandths
33. 5;8;8;7;1;2;3;five hundred eighty-eight and seven thousand one hundred
    twenty-three ten-thousandths
34. 5;4;2;3;0;0;0;0;5;6;five thousand, four hundred twenty-three and fifty-
    six millionths

Learning Unit 1.2

Rounding and Approximations

1. 26,490; 26,500; 26,000
2. 193,830; 193,800; 194,000
3. 7,140; 7,100; 7,000
4. 14,930; 14,900; 15,000
5. 1,860; 1,900; 2,000
6. 683,000; 680,000; 700,000
7. 327,000; 330,000; 300,000
8. 774,000; 770,000; 800,000
9. 150,000; 150,000; 100,000
10. 574,000; 570,000; 600,000
11. 79,000,000
12. 12,000,000
13. 3,000,000
14. 8,000,000
15. 77; 76.8; 76.83
16. 3; 2.7; 2.65
17. 9; 9.4; 9.44
18. 4; 3.7; 3.67
19. 5; 5.4; 5.43

20. .64; .644
21. .39; .394
22. 7.54; 7.542
23. 13.65; 13.653
24. .49; .493

Learning Unit 1.3

Addition and Subtraction

of Whole Numbers

1.   1,247   2.   907   3.   17   4.   723
     13,488   1,326   133   1,422
     +   344   +18,945   +1,904   +1,036
     ------   -------   ------   ------
     15,079   21,178   2,054   3,181

5.   29   6.   73   7.   333   8.   448
       86   29   672   621
       31   36   135   381
       +44   +74   899   317
       ---   ---   +216   +495
       190   212   -----   -----
                                              2,255   2,262

9.   342   10.   924   11.   382   12.   140
       734   652   149   376
       584 1,660   370 1,946   661 1,192   894 1,410
       521   503   724   502
       935   479   382   468
       754 2,210   830 1,812   974 2,080   249 1,219
       606   215   506   791
       419   146   293   610
       +197 1,222   +307   668   810   485
       -----   ----- ---   +421 2,030   +904 2,790
       5,092   4,426   -----   -----
                                              5,302   5,419

13.   397   14.   892   15.   762   16.   5,488
       -256   -376   -575   -3,257
       ----   ----   ----   ------
       141   516   187   2,231

17.   7,253   18.   3,136   19.   18,759   20.   39,302
      -2,567   -2,749   - 6,247   -12,736
      ------   ------   -------   -------
       4,686   387   12,512   26,566

21.   41,424   22.   54,521   23.   105,624 24.   157,309
     - 7,589   -12,375   - 3,731   - 44,632
     -------   -------   --------   --------
      33,835   42,146   101,893   112,677

25. 346 - 32 = 314
26. 9,728 - 539 = 9,189
27. 8,655 - 364 = 8,291
28. 10,233 - 1,145 = 9,088
29. 29,342 - 18,778 = 10,564
30. 16,779 - 7,886 = 8,893
31. $862 - $427 - $34 = $401
32. $605 - $148 - $121 = $336
33. $998 + $673 - $186 = $1,485
34. $322 + $298 - $428 = $192
35. $1,605 - $413 + $219 = $1,411
36. $1,064 - $872 + $987 = $1,179

37. $6,741 + $692 - $745 = $6,688
38. $3,208 + $570 - $391 = $3,387
39. 462 + 347 + 512 + 391 + 427 = 2,139
40. 98 + 106 + 113 + 107 + 117 = 541
41. 732 + 640 + 756 + 710 + 684 = 3,522
42. 103 + 86 + 108 + 116 + 114 = 527
43. 219 + 273 + 314 + 221 + 306 = 1,333
44. $1,240 + 1,765 + 1,872 + 1,136 + 1,307 = $7,320
45. $348 + 634 + 506 + 722 + 512 = $2,722
46. $1,866 + 1,292 + 1,460 + 1,756 + 1,424 = $7,798
47. $3,454 + 3,691 + 3,838 + 3,614 + 3,243 = $17,840
48. $942 - 567 = $375
49. $168 - 87 = $81
50. $6,347 - 3,238 = $3,109
51. $3,063 - 1,607 = $1,456

Learning Unit 1.4

Multiplication and Division

of Whole Numbers

1.	4,970 x 31 154,070	2.	3,205 x 16 51,280	3.	7,614 x 24 182,736	4.	5,089 x 76 386,764
5.	1,898 x 575 1,091,350	6.	8,924 x 896 7,995,904	7.	2,945 x 854 2,515,030	8.	36,054 x 396 14,277,384
9.	45,806 x 427 19,559,162	10.	74,683 x 787 58,775,521	11.	80,249 x 363 29,130,387	12.	39,625 x 706 27,975,250
13.	147,892 x 300 44,367,600	14.	532,300 x 160 85,168,000	15.	305,076 x 885 269,992,260	16.	308,207 x 275 84,756,925

17. 372 x 45 - 467 = 16,273
18. 185 x 39 - 512 = 6,703
19. 643 x 762 - 897 = 489,069
20. 459 x 188 - 632 = 85,660
21. 2,488/22 = 113;2
22. 4,605/54 = 85;15
23. 1,876/31 = 60;16
24. 5,647/68 = 83;3
25. 2,672/154 = 17;54
26. 7,083/344 = 20;203
27. 17,396/407 = 42;302
28. 29,107/326 = 89;93
29. 14,252/176 = 80;172
30. 23,931/324 = 73;279
31. 496 x 54 = 26,784
32. 721 x 23 = 16,583
33. 384 x 78 = 29,952
34. 587 x 68 = 39,916
35. 789 x 39 = 30,771
36. 923 x 28 = 25,844

37. 327 x 63 = 20,601
38. 382 x 147 = 56,154
39. 48 x 14 = 672 miles
40. $72 x 35 = $2,520
41. 6 x $18 =   (a) $108.00
    12 x $11 =   132.00
    5 x $29 =   145.00
    19 x $28 =   532.00
                 (b) $917.00

42. 1,575/225 = 7 hours
43. $216/36 = $6
44. 560/14 = 40 hours

Learning Unit 1.5

Addition and Subtraction

of Decimal Numbers

1.   1.045
       7.231
       8.104
       5.742
       6.208
     + 1.901
      30.231
      30.23

2.   5.081
       1.707
       6.014
       1.624
       1.002
     + 4.682
      20.110
      20.11

3.   2.09
       1.706
       3.1
       4.106
       3.164
     + 7.772
      21.938
      21.94

4. $172.50
      95.20
     297.14
      13.90
     105.50
    +   3.47
    $687.71

5.   4.805
      13.8
        .6061
      17.401
      22.63
    +125
     184.2421
     184.24

6.   1.6
      34.021
      11.4
     176.1
      98.774
    + 33.3967
     355.2917
     355.29

7. $ 14.98
       788.62
       590.00
        50.38
        10.49
    + 865.07
    $2,319.54

8.   .5602
        69.2
       480
         4.6405
        12.209
    + 926.44
     1,493.0497
     1,493.05

9.   36.1
         9.7763
       259
        33.89
       444.6762
    +1,233
     2,016.4425
     2,016.44

10.   4.27
      -1.643
       2.627
       2.63

11. $159.06
    - 73.40
    $ 85.66

12.   1.343
      -1.279
        .064
        .06

13.   1.002
      - .1432
        .8588
        .86

14. $99.10
    -73.69
    $25.41

15.   9.1275
      -6.139
       2.9885
       2.99

16.	259.1769	17.	495.881	18.	1,642.34
	- 93.407		-158.7729		- 692.366
	165.7699		337.1081		949.974
	165.77		337.11		949.97

19. .065 + 4.1365 + 1.01 + .0014 = 5.2129
    1.17 + .715 + 2.006 + .104 = 3.995
    5.2129 - 3.995 = 1.2179 = 1.22

20. $76.47 + 17.26 = $93.73
21. $47.50 - 12.32 = $35.18
22. $3,400 - 2,146.76 = $1,253.24
23. $179.95 - 132 = $47.95
24. $4.98 + 6.02 + 5.19 + .81 = $17
    $20 - 17 = $3

25. $87.00 + 11.29 + 762.40 = $860.69
    $860.69 - 200 = $660.69

26. $348.12 + 87.25 + 1,482.68 = $1,918.05
    $1,918.05 - 226 = -$1,692.05

Learning Unit 1.6

Multiplication and Division

of Decimal Numbers

1.	4.02	2.	7.09	3.	1.227
	x1.17		x.062		x .61
	4.7034		.43958		.74847
	4.70		.44		.75

4.	5.162	5.	$ 99.08	6.	34.19
	x 93		x1.304		x11.93
	480.066		$129.20032		407.8867
	480.07		$129.20		407.89

7.	1.456	8.	46.93	9.	76.45
	x 1.2		x.0761		x 3.75
	1.7472		3.571373		286.6875
	1.75		3.57		286.69

10. 2.51)45.89.300   → 18.28 / 18.284
11. 1.45)60.14.000   → 41.48 / 41.475
12. .57)8.99.700   → 15.78 / 15.784

13. .229)34.260.000   → 149.61 / 149.606
14. 1.19)90.43.260   → 75.99 / 75.993
15. $9.65)$1,237.00.000   → $128.19 / $128.186

16. 49.87)8.83.500   → .18 / .177
17. 123.1).8.826   → .01 / .007
18. 23.71)10,009.00.000   → 422.14 / 422.142

19. 372 x 10 = 3,720
20. 7.2 x 10 = 72
21. 9.6 x 100 = 960
22. 86 x 100 = 8,600
23. .36 x 100 = 36
24. 9.8 x 1,000 = 9,800

25. 3.6 x 40 = 144
27. 963 x 100 = 96,300
29. 67 x 20 = 1,340
31. 550 x 30 = 16,500
33. 9.55 x 50 = 477.5
35. 920 x 60 = 55,200
37. .79 x 2,000 = 1,580
39. 45.9/10 = 4.59
41. 14,654/1000 = 14.654
43. 420/25 = 16.8
45. 368/100 = 3.68
47. 768/1,000 = .768
49. 6.2/10 = .62
51. $160/25 = $6.40
53. 3,249/1,000 = 3.249
55. $3,420/2,000 = $1.71
57. 5,46/100 = .0546

26. 25 x 100 = 2,500
28. 92 x 30 = 2,760
30. 6.5 x 50 = 325
32. 162 x 25 = 4,050
34. 175 x 40 = 7,000
36. 24.28 x 25 = 607
38. 7.94 x 50 = 397
40. 76/100 = .76
42. 9.21/10 = .921
44. .26/10 = .026
46. .05/100 = .0005
48. $7.60/10 = $.76
50. 800/500 = 1.6
52. $160/100 = $1.60
54. 280/40 = 7
56. 275.1/30 = 9.17
58. 17.5/25 = .7

59. 2,746 x $1.88 = $5,162.48
60. $17,675/14 = $1,262.50
61. 768 x $.185 = $142.08
62. 92 x .125 = 11.5 pounds
63. $14.875 + .15 = $15.025
    $15.025 x 75 = $1,126.875 = $1,126.88

64. $14.875 + .15 = $15.025
    $1,202/15.025 = 80 shares

65. 12 x $.24 = $2.88

Chapter 1
Self-Evaluation

1. 124,357
2. six and five thousand four ten-thousandths
3. 133.16; 548.3; 4.224
4. 3,402 + 18,961 + 340,265 = 362,628
5. 1,742 - 396 = 1,346
6. 31,482 - 16,539 = 14,943
7. $103,000 + 1,542 + 312 + 1,400 = $106,254
8. $463,282 - 274,406 = $188,876
9. 34.2567 + 122.3 + 4.333 + 36.23 = 197.1197
10. 244.5 - 34.9621 = 209.5379

11. 13.453 + 162.3265 + .8132 = 176.5927
    .354 + 15.76 + 8.3647 = 24.4787
    176.5927 - 24.4787 = 152.114

12. 53.65/3.7 = 14.5
13. 23 x $6.95 = $159.85

Chapter 2

Fractions

A. Purpose

This chapter provides the student an opportunity to review the fundamental
operations of arithmetic involving fractions. Primary emphasis is given to
the processes for converting fractions to other forms for easier solutions
to business problems.

B. Comments

1. Reducing fractions to lowest terms can be a hazardous "guessing game"
    at times. Finding the greatest common divisor, as shown in Learning
    Unit 2.1, will eliminate all "guessing."
2. Some emphasis should be given to the terminology associated with the
    various types of fractions to make discussion easier for students.
3. Factoring prime numbers, as presented in Learning Unit 2.3, eliminates
    "guessing" in finding the lowest common denominator of fractions to be
    added or subtracted.

C. Solutions

Learning Unit 2.1

Changing the Terms

of Fractions

1. $9/15 = 3/5$ ($\div 3$)   2. $28/36 = 7/9$ ($\div 4$)   3. $45/75 = 3/5$ ($\div 15$)
4. $35/49 = 5/7$ ($\div 7$) 5. $57/76 = 3/4$ ($\div 19$) 6. $126/190 = 63/95$ ($\div 2$)
7. $18/53$ 8. $320/448 = 5/7$ ($\div 64$) 9. $210/546 = 5/13$ ($\div 42$)

10. 265/477 =
    5/9 (÷ 53)
11. 315/560 =
    9/16 (÷ 35)
12. 528/716 =
    132/179 (÷ 4)
13. 1,221/1,998 =
    11/18 (÷ 111)
14. 452/761
15. 511/876 =
    7/12 (÷ 73)
16. 2/3 = 8/12
17. 5/6 = 15/18
18. 3/8 = 18/48
19. 7/9 = 49/63
20. 4/9 = 36/81
21. 5/12 = 65/156
22. 4/5 = 108/135
23. 3/4 = 102/136
24. 12/21 = 180/315
25. 3/10 = 66/220
26. 11/12 = 473/516
27. 29/65 = 348/780
28. 1/4 = 12/48
29. 3/8 = 18/48
30. 5/16 = 15/48
31. 19/24 = 38/48
32. 7/12 = 28/48
33. 2/3 = 32/48

Learning Unit 2.2

Improper Fractions, Mixed

Numbers, and Decimals

1. 5/2 = 2 1/2
2. 9/4 = 2 1/4
3. 37/6 = 6 1/6
4. 59/12 = 4 11/12
5. 69/4 = 17 1/4
6. 117/8 = 14 5/8
7. 97/30 = 3 7/30
8. 210/25 = 8 2/5
9. 6 1/2 = (2 x 6 + 1)/2
   = 13/2
10. 3 4/7 = 25/7
11. 6 3/8 = 51/8
12. 9 7/16 = 151/16
13. 4 11/12 = 59/12
14. 8 3/11 = 91/11
15. 14 13/20 = 293/20
16. 26 19/24 = 643/24
17. 3/5 = .6
18. 12 5/8 = 12.625
19. 5/6 = .833
20. 8 7/12 = 8.583
21. 9/16 = .563
22. 5/9 = .556
23. 26 29/40 = 26.725
24. 41/250 = .164
25. 0.7 = 7/10
26. 4.75 = 4 3/4
27. 0.65 = 13/20
28. 0.875 = 7/8
29. 18.025 = 18 1/40
30. 0.0025 = 1/400
31. 3.250 = 3 1/4
32. 4.352 = 4 44/125

Learning Unit 2.3

Addition and Subtraction

of Fractions

1. 3/5 + 4/10 + 1/2 =
   6/10 + 4/10 + 5/10 = 15/10 = 1 1/2
2. 6 2/9 + 2/3 + 1 1/5 = 8 4/45
3. 7 3/4 + 18 7/10 + 4 1/2 = 30 19/20
4. 11 4/9 + 5/18 + 8 3/4 = 20 17/36
5. 5/8 + 3 7/9 + 2 5/6 = 7 17/72
6. 17 3/5 + 6 1/8 + 12 4/7 = 36 83/280
7. 7/10 - 1/5 = 7/10 - 2/10 = 1/2
8. 3 11/12 - 2 2/3 = 1 1/4
9. 43 1/4 - 17 3/15 = 26 1/20
10. 9 7/12 - 6 1/3 = 3 1/4
11. 5 1/9 - 3 1/10 = 2 1/90
12. 13/18 - 1/12 = 23/36
13. 5/9 + 1/3 + 1/2 + 8/15 = 1 83/90
14. 2/3 - 7/12 - 2/5 + 5/6 = 31/60
15. 1/9 + 2/3 - 2/5 - 1/4 = 23/180
16. 5/6 - 1/3 + 3/4 - 3/5 = 13/20
17. 19 2/3 - 4 1/2 - 7 1/5 = 7 29/30
18. 26 7/12 - 18 2/3 + 3 5/6 = 11 3/4
19. 46 1/2 + 13 2/3 + 7 3/8 + 9 + 1 5/8 = 78 1/6
20. 4 1/4 - 2 5/6 = 1 5/12
21. 246 1/2 - (19 1/8 + 21 1/4 + 17 7/10 + 24 1/2) = 163 37/40
22. 109 1/16 - 86 7/8 = 22 3/16

Learning Unit 2.4

Multiplication and Division

of Fractions

1. 1/2 x 4/9 = 4/18 = 2/9
2. 1/6 x 3/8 = 1/16
3. 5/16 x 8/9 x 6/7 = 5/21
4. 9/32 x 17/21 x 11/15 = 187/1,120

5. 7 x 5 1/6 = 7/1 x 31/6
               = 217/6
               = 36 1/6

6. 2 3/8 x 4 1/7 = 9 47/56

7. 17 1/5 x 2 2/3 = 45 13/15

8. 1 3/5 x 3 1/4 x 1 1/15 = 5 41/75

9. 1/4 x 4/9 x 5/16 x 4/15 = 1/108

10. 8 x 4 1/3 x 2 2/5 = 83 1/5

11. 5/8 ÷ 11/16 = 5/8 x 16/11 = 10/11

12. 1/6 ÷ 11/15 = 5/22

13. 3/5 ÷ 4/5 = 3/4

14. 18 ÷ 2/3 = 27

15. 4 5/8 ÷ 9 1/2 = 37/76

16. 16 1/2 ÷ 14 = 1 5/28

17. 8 2/3 ÷ 4/9 ÷ 6 = 3 1/4

18. 15 2/3 ÷ 3 3/4 ÷ 1/8 = 33 19/45

19. 17 5/8 ÷ 16 5/12 = 1 29/394

20. 9 7/8 ÷ 9 1/4 = 1 5/74

21. 1/12 x $696/1 = $58

22. $36 ÷ 3/5 = $60

23. $55,440 x 1/3 = $18,480
    $55,440 x 1/4 = $13,860
    $55,440 x 5/12 = $23,100

24. $268 ÷ 3/5 = $446.67

25. 12 3/8 x 9 1/6 = 113 7/16

26. $2.87 ÷ 7/12 = $4.92

Chapter 2
Self-Evaluation

1. 52/78 = 2/3

2. 1/4 = 9/36

3. 3/8 = 9/24

4. 39/4 = 9 3/4

5. 7 1/4 = (4 x 7 + 1)/4 = 29/4

6. 1/4 = 1 ÷ 4 = .25

7. .75 = 75/100 = 3/4

8. 2)8̸ 6̸ 4̸   2 x 2 x 2 x 3 = 24
    2)4̸ 3 2̸
       2 3 1

9. 3/4 − 1/3 = 9/12 − 4/12 = 5/12

10. 2/3̸1 x 3̸1/6̸3 x 3̸1/3̸1 = 1/3

11. 5 1/3 ÷ 2 1/4
    = 16/3 ÷ 9/4
    = 16/3 x 4/9 = 64/27
    = 2 10/27

12. $12 3/8 x 15
    = 99/8 x 15/1
    = 1,485/8
    = $185.63

13. 84/1 ÷ 3/4
    = 84/1 x 4/3
    = 336/3
    = 112

Chapter 3

Percents

A.   Purpose

This chapter acquaints the student with the use of percents. Primary emphasis is given to the processes for converting percents to fractions and decimals in order to solve business problems.

B.   Comments

1.   Converting percents to fractions or decimals will be easier for stu-
     dents if they understand that "percent means hundredths."
2.   Solving equations seems to cause many students a great deal of concern.
     The percentage formula in Learning Unit 3.3 might be best presented as
     a "helpful tool" to solve all types of business and day-to-day problems.

C.   Solutions

Learning Unit 3.1

Converting Decimals,

Fractions, and Percents

 1.   3% = .03.% = .03   2.   .07   3.   .36   4.   .45
 5.   .273   6.   .589   7.   .1406   8.   .7299
 9.   .135   10.   .275   11.   .2625   12.   .1875
13.   .005   14.   .0025   15.   1.97   16.   3.05
17.   .9632   18.   .5408   19.   2.737   20.   4.0684
21.   .04 =   .04.% = 4%   22.   35%   23.   520%   24.   1700%
25.   2.2%   26.   12.5%   27.   900%   28.   130.52%

29. 33 1/3%   30.   .8 1/4%   31.   20%   32.   200%
33. 42.06%   34. 600.3%   35.   525%   36.   214%
37. 3700%   38. 89.2%   39. 1326%   40.   370.2%
41. 10% = 10/100 = 1/10   42.   3 3/4   43.   2/175   44.   29/40
45. 2 81/500   46. 1/250   47. 4/25   48. 46/125
49. 3/400   50. 181/50,000   51. 1/4   52. 1 43/100
53. 1/500   54. 6/25   55. 9/400   56. 2 1/4
57. 1/2   58. 1/800   59. 1/200   60. 3 1/25
61. 1/3 = .33.33 = 33.33% = 33 1/3%   62.   325%
63. 20%   64. 75%   65. 1710%   66. 16.67%
67. 87.5%   68. 37.5%   69. 570%   70. 115%
71. 262.5%   72. 137.5%   73. 106.25%   74. 80%
75. 75%   76. 52%   77. 1820%   78. 10%
79. 12.5%   80. 60%
81. .5, 50%   82. 1/4, 25%   83. .20, 20%   84. 3/10, .30
85. 2 9/20, 245%   86. 3/4, .75   87. 2.75, 275%   88. 36 2/5, 3640%
89. 31/200, .155   90. .625, 62.5%
91. 80/1 x $1/16 = $Ø5/1 x $1/Ø1 = $5
92. 1500 x $.05 = $75   93. 420 x $.14 2/7 = $60
94. 810 x $.11 1/9 = $90   95. 600 x $.16 2/3 = $100

Learning Unit 3.2

Solving Equations

1. $a + 7 = 21$
      $a + 7 - 7 = 21 - 7$
           $a = 14$

2. $c - 3 = 7$
           $c = 10$

3. $b/3 = 3$
      $3/1 \cdot b/3 = 3 \cdot 3$
                $b = 9$

4. $4c = 12$
       $c = 3$

5. $2/a = 7$
       $a = 2/7$

6. $7 - b = 3$
          $b = 4$

7. $4 + c = 11$
          $c = 7$

8. $8m = 32$
       $m = 4$

9. $r + 2 = 7$
          $r = 5$

10. $a/21 = 3$
          $a = 63$

11. $b - 3 = 17$
          $b = 20$

12. $6c = 3$
       $c = 1/2$

13. $5a = 7$
       $a = 1\ 2/5$

14. $y - 9 = 1$
          $y = 10$

15. $x + 1/2 = 2/3$
          $x = 1/6$

16. $.25c = 3$
          $c = 12$

17. $\dfrac{b}{\frac{1}{2}} = 7$
      $b = 7/2 = 3\ 1/2$

18. $a - .17 = 3.2$
          $a = 3.37$

19. $3\ 1/2\ x = 7$
          $x = 2$

20. $a/.2 = 6$
          $a = 1.2$

Learning Unit 3.3

Finding Parts,

Base, and Rate

1. $P = B \times R$
     $P = 72 \times .2$
     $P = 14.4$

2. $P = 2.25$

3. $P = .035$

4. $\underline{R} = P/B = 3/9 = 1/3 = 33\ 1/3\%$ 5. $\underline{R} = 25\%$ 6. $\underline{R} = 150\%$
7. $\underline{B} = P/R = 20/.08 = 250$ 8. $\underline{B} = 51$ 9. $\underline{B} = 100$
10. $\underline{P} = 1.6$ 11. $\underline{P} = 6$ 12. $\underline{R} = 25\%$
13. $\underline{R} = 20\%$ 14. $\underline{B} = 500$ 15. $\underline{B} = 1,200$
16. $\$304,265 \times .07 = \$21,298.55$ 17. $\$42,000 \div .20 = \$210,000$
18. (a) $\$275 \times .15 = \$41.25$ (b) $\$41.25 + \$275 = \$316.25$
19. $156 \times .61 = 95$ 20. $\$21.40 \times .05 = \$1.07$
21. (a) $\$11/.10 = \$110$ (b) $\$110 - \$11 = \$99$
22. $442 \div 613 = .72 = 72\%$ 23. $\$150/.20 = \$750$
24. $\$336,000/\$420,000 = 80\%$
25. $\$30,000 \times .03 = \$\ \ \ 900$ 26. $6,200 \times .07 = 434$
    $\$13,254 \times .05 = \$\ \ \ 662.70$ $6,200 - 434 = 5,766$
    $\overline{\ \ \$1,562.70\ \ }$

27. $\$150 \times .04 = \$6$ 28. $18 - 15 = 3$
    $\$150 + \$6 = \$156$ $3/18 = 16.67\%$
29. $\$40/.05 = \$800$ 30. $5/40 = 1/8 = 12\ 1/2\%$
31. $\$10,000 \times .75 = \$7,500$ 32. $7/25 = 28\%$
33. $50/285 = 17.54\%$ 34. $\underline{B} = P/R = \$350/.60 = \$583.33$
35. $\$172/.07 = \$2,457.14$ 36. $\$1,575 \times 1.1 = \$1,732.50$
37. $\$525/\$1,078 = 48.72\%$ 38. $\$9,000/\$51,000 = 13.73\%$
39. $\$17,500/.05 = \$350,000$ 40. $\$225 \times .38 = \$85.50$

Chapter 3
Self-Evaluation

1. $29\% = .29$
2. $.355 = 35.5\%$
3. $25\% = .25 = 25/100 = 1/4$
4. $3\ 1/5 = 3.2 = 320\%$
5. $\underline{P} = .03 \times \$120.00 = \$3.60$
6. $60 = \underline{R} \times 240; \ 60/240 = \underline{R}; \ 1/4 = \underline{R}; \ 25\% = \underline{R}$
7. $\underline{P} = I/(\underline{R} \times \underline{T}); \ \underline{P} = \dfrac{\$72}{\dfrac{6}{100} \times \dfrac{1}{1}}; \ \underline{P} = 72/1 \times 100/6; \ \underline{P} = \$1,200$
8. $5 = \underline{R} \times 25; \ 5/25 = \underline{R}; \ 1/5 = \underline{R}; \ 20\% = \underline{R}$
9. $\underline{P} = 1.05 \times \$12.95; \ \underline{P} = \$13.28$
10. $68 = \underline{R} \times 3,400; \ 68/3,400 = \underline{R}; \ 2\% = \underline{R}$
11. $\underline{P} = .05 \times \$52,000; \ \underline{P} = \$2,600$
12. $\$60,000 = .90 \times \underline{B}; \ \$60,000/.90 = \underline{B}; \ \$66,667 = \underline{B}$
13. $3\underline{B} = 12; \ \underline{B} = 12/3 = 4$
14. $\underline{B} - 7 = 10; \ \underline{B} = 10 + 7; \ \underline{B} = 17$
15. $\$.0625 \times 320 = \$20.00$

Chapter 4

Trade Pricing

A. Purpose

This chapter explains two of the most common commercial discounts--trade
discounts and cash discounts. Both types of trade discounts (single discounts and chain discounts) are covered, as is the method for computing
partial payments. The process for determining the net decimal equivalent
of the percent paid and the single discount equivalent for chain discounts
is explained.

B. Comments

1. Several terms presented in this chapter are not familiar to many stu-
    dents and should be explained and illustrated by the instructor.
2. The fact that a cash discount does not apply to returned goods or
    transportation charges should be given special emphasis.
3. The process for computing the amount of credit on partial payments
    made within the cash discount period should be stressed, especially
    the reason for granting more credit than the amount of the partial
    payment.

C. Solutions

Learning Unit 4.1

Trade Discounts

1. 100% - 43% = 57% = .57   2. $786 x .7 = $550.20
    $90 x .57 = $51.30
3. $650 x .76 = $494   4. $647 x .54 = $349.38
5. $936 x .66667 = $624   6. $6.36 x .8333 = $5.30

7. $36.24 x .68 = $24.64

8. $95.44 x .59 = $56.31

9. $48.48 x .875 = $42.42

10. $33.93 x .66667 = $22.62

11. .75 x .8 = .6
    $192.40 x .6 = $115.44

12. .8 x .9 = .72
    $72.30 x .72 = $52.06

13. .7 x .9 x .9 = .567
    $196 x .567 = $111.13

14. .65 x .8 x .95 = .494
    $45.20 x .494 = $22.33

15. .8 x .8 x .9 = .576
    $114.10 x .576 = $65.72

16. .8 x .9 x .9 = .648
    $221.80 x .648 = $143.73

17. 100% - 20% = 80% or .8
    100% - 10% = 90% or .9
    .8 x .9 = .72
    1.00 - .72 = .28 = 28%

18. .8 x .7 = .56
    1.00 - .56 = .44 = 44%

19. .7 x .9 x .9 = .567
    1.00 - .567 = .433 = 43.3%

20. .75 x .8 x .9 = .54
    1.00 - .54 = .46 = 46%

21. .6 x .95 x .95 = .5415
    1.00 - .5415 = .4585 = 46%

22. .65 x .9 x .95 = .55575
    1.00 - .55575 = .44425 = 44%

23. .7 x .9 = .63
    .8 x .8 = .64

24. .67 x .85 = .5695
    .75 x .8 = .6

25. .8 x .85 x .9 = .612
    .75 x .8 = .6

26. .85 x .9 x .95 = .72675
    .8 x .9 = .72

27. 100% - 30% = 70% = .7
    $299.95 x .7 = $209.97

28. .7 x .9 x .9 = .567
    $37.99 x .567 = $21.54

29. (a) .7 x .8 = .56
        $319.95 x .56 = $179.17
    (b) $179.17 + 14.79 = $193.96

30. (a) .55 x .8 = .44
        $1,640 x .44 = $721.60
    (b) $721.60 + $53.20 = $774.80

31. (a) .7 x .8 x .9 = .504
        $278 x .504 = $140.11
    (b) $278 - $140.11 = $137.89

32. .6 x .8 = .48
    1 - .48 = .52
    $730 x .52 = $379.60
    $730 - $379.60 = $350.40

33. .7 x .9 x .9 = .567
    $96 x 5 = $480
    $480 x .567 = $272.16

34. (a) .85 x .85 x .9 = .65025
        $39.95 x .65025 = $25.98
    (b) .8 x .85 = .68
        $39.95 x .68 = $27.17

35. (a) .7 x .9 x .95 = .5985
        $29.95 x .5985 = $17.93
        .8 x .8 x .9·= .576
        $28.95 x .576 = $16.68
    (b) $17.93 - $16.68 = $1.25

36. .9 x .95 x .95 = .81225
    $34.95 x .81225 = $28.39

Learning Unit 4.2

Cash Discounts

1. $378.56 x .98 = $370.99
2. $762.18 x .99 = $754.56
3. $613.42 x .97 = $595.02
4. $77.98 x .98 = $76.42
5. $946.34
6. $422.61 x .98 = $414.16

7. $806.52 x .98 = $790.39   8. $235.10
9. $86.48 x .99 = $85.62   10. $316.98 x .98 = $310.64
11. $189.23   12. $544.55 x .98 = $533.66
13. (a) October 2 plus 10 days = October 12
    (b) 31 - 2 = 29 days in October
                 1 day in November (November 1)
14. (a) August 7 plus 10 days = August 17
    (b) 31 - 7 = 24 days in August
          60 - 24 = 36 days remaining
             - 30 = days in September
                 6 days in October (October 6)
15. (a) May 10   (b) May 25
16. (a) July 13   (b) August 27
17. (a) March 31   (b) June 19
18. (a) June 10   (b) August 24
19. $197.10 - $20 - $7.10 = $170 amount subject to the cash discount
    $170 x .02 = $3.40 cash discount
    $170 - $3.40 + $7.10 = $173.70 payment
20. $4.20 cash discount
    $211.97 payment
21. $24 cash discount
    $586 payment
22. $15.60 cash discount
    $523.40 payment
23. $346.24 - $26.24 = $320 amount subject to the cash discount
    $320 x .03 = $9.60 cash discount
    $320 - $9.60 = $310.40 payment
24. $17.40 cash discount
    $852.60 payment
25. $9.24 cash discount
    $452.76 payment
26. $10.05 cash discount
    $324.95 payment
27. $150/.98 = $153.06 credit
    $322.40 - $153.06 = $169.34 amount outstanding
28. $231.96 credit
    $222.39 amount outstanding
29. $434.34 credit
    $483.76 amount outstanding
30. $877.55 credit
    $379.35 amount outstanding
31. $180.41 credit
    $219.46 amount outstanding
32. $1,020.41 credit
    $969.35 amount outstanding
33. (a) $16.95 x .45 = $7.63 trade price
    (b) $7.63 x .98 = $7.48 net cost
34. 30 - 14 = 16 days in June
    60 - 16 = 44 days remaining
             -31 days in July
              13 days in August (August 13)

35. 30 - 24 = 6 days in September
    90 - 6 = 84 days remaining
             -31 days in October
              53 days remaining
             -30 days in November
              23 days in December (December 23)

36. (a) 31 - 16 = 15 days in March
        30 - 15 = 15 days in April (April 15)
    (b) March 16 + 10 days = March 26
    (c) $368 x .03 = $11.04
37. (a) 31 - 18 = 13 days in October
        30 - 13 = 17 days in November (November 17)
    (b) October 18 + 5 days = October 23
    (c) $274
    (d) $274 x .98 = $268.52
38. $299.67 x .98 = $293.68
39. $264.22 - $24.12 - $10.10 = $230 amount subject to cash discount
    $230 x .01 = $2.30 cash discount
    $230 - $2.30 + $10.10 = $237.80 amount owed on September 23
40. $146.82 - $18.74 = $128.08 amount subject to the cash discount
    $128.08 x .02 = $2.56 cash discount
    $128.08 - $2.56 + $18.74 = $144.26 amount paid
41. (a) July 16 + 10 days = July 26
    (b) 31 - 16 = 15 days in July
        30 - 15 = 15 days in August (August 15)
42. (a) $940 x .02 = $18.80
    (b) 60 - 15 = 45 days
43. (a) yes
    (b) 30 - 10 = 20 days
    (c) $310 x .02 = $6.20 cash discount
        $6.20 - $1.35 = $4.85 amount saved
44. $550/.98 = $561.22 credit
45. (a) $150/.97 = $154.64 credit for the partial payment
    (b) $327 - $154.64 = $172.36 amount outstanding

Chapter 4
Self- Evaluation

1. $649 x .73 = $473.77

2. $55.80 x .62 = $34.60

3. .8 x .9 = .72
    .85 x .85 = .7225
    The 20%, 10% chain discount is better.

4. .7 x .8 x .9 = .504
    .8 x .8 x .8 = .512
    The 30%, 20%, 10% chain discount is better.

5. .8 x .9 x .9 = .648 single discount equivalent
    $164 x .648 = $106.27 trade price

6. .85 x .9 = .765 single discount equivalent
    $204.60 x .765 = $156.52 trade price

7. $327.60 x .02 = $6.55 cash discount
    $327.60 - $6.55 = $321.05 payment

8. $144.76 x .02 = $2.90 cash discount
    $144.76 - $2.90 = $141.86 payment

18

9. $186.50 - $6.50 - $20 = $160 amount subject to the cash discount
$160 x .04 = $6.40 cash discount
$160 - $6.40 + $6.50 = $160.10 payment

10. $860.40 - $10.40 - $40 = $810 amount subject to the cash discount
$810 x .03 = $24.30 cash discount
$810 - $24.30 + $10.40 = $796.10 payment

11. $450/.98 = $459.18 credit
$891.60 - $459.18 = $432.42 outstanding balance

Chapter 5

Retail Pricing

A. Purpose

The retail price of an item must be calculated so that the seller will re-
cover the cost of the item itself, the expenses involved in selling the
item, and a desired amount of profit. Chapter 5 is designed to present
pricing procedures and information for retail price determination.

B. Comments

1. Markon can be calculated using the relationships introduced by the percentage formula in Chapter 3, where

   $$\frac{M}{C} = Part \qquad or \qquad \frac{M}{R} = Part$$
   $$C = Base \qquad\qquad R = Base$$
   $$C\% = Rate \qquad\qquad R\% = Rate$$

2. The diagram at the end of Learning Unit 5.1 illustrates the relation-
   ship of the markon formulas and how they are used in combination to
   solve retail pricing problems.
3. Seasonal or perishable goods are priced differently from most retail
   items and, therefore, are presented in a separate learning unit.
4. Final prices for seasonal or perishable goods--especially fast food
   items--may vary from the actual price as it is mathematically determined. Many items have "generally accepted prices"; i.e., a pizza
   that should sell for $3.14 may sell for $2.99, $3.19, or $3.29.

20

C. Solutions

Learning Unit 5.1
Markon Based on
Cost and Retail

1. $R = C + M$ 2. $160.00   3. $190.00   4. $65.00
    $R = 123 + 82$
    $R = 205$

5. $R = C + M$ 6. $96.00   7. $114.00   8. $39.00
    $R - M = C$
    $205 - 82 = C$
    $123 = C$

9. $R = C + M$ 10. $64.00   11. $76.00   12. $26.00
    $R - C = M$
    $205 - 123 = M$
    $82 = M$

13. $M = C \times C\%$ or $R = C + M$
     $M = 9.90 \times .50$ $R = 100\%C + 50\%C$
     $M = 4.95$ $R = 150\%C$
     $R = C + M$ $R = 1.50 \times 9.90$
     $R = 9.90 + 4.95$ $R = 14.85$
     $R = 14.85$

14. $13.35   15. $10.10   16. $20.92   17. $20.41

18. $19.13   19. $R = C + M$ 20. $6.48   21. $6.64
              $R = 100\%C + 53\%C$
              $R = 153\%C$
              $R/1.53 = C$
              $22.84/1.53 = C$
              $14.93 = C$

22. $18.78   23. $7.35   24. $8.62   25. $R = C + M$
                                            $R - C = M$
                                            $17.23 - 11.80 = M$
                                            $5.43 = M$
                                            $C\% = M/C$
                                            $= 5.43/11.80$
                                            $= .4602 = 46.02\%$

26. $5.80, 46.03%   27. $3.82, 35.05%   28. $3.92, 35.00%

29. $3.90, 25.00%   30. $3.50, 25.00%

31. $R = C + M$ 32. $17.80
     $100\%R = C + 50\%R$
     $50\%R = C$
     $R = C/.50 = 9.90/.50 = 19.80$

33. $26.54   34. $23.65   35. $22.16   36. $43.08

37. $R = C + M$ or $M = R \times R\%$
    $100\%R = C + 53\%R$ $M = \$22.84 \times .53$
    $47\%R = C$ $M = \$12.11$
    $.47 \times \$22.84 = C$ $R = C + M$
    $\$10.73 = C$ $R - M = C$
                       $\$22.84 - \$12.11 = C$
                       $\$10.73 = C$

38. $3.83   39. $4.98   40. $6.93   41. $7.00

42. $7.68   43. $R = C + M$
                  $R - C = M$
                  $\$17.23 - \$11.80 = M$
                  $\$5.43 = M$
                  $R\% = M/R = \$5.43/\$17.23 = .3151 = 31.51\%$

44. $5.80, 31.52%   45. $3.82, 25.95%   46. $3.92, 25.93%

47. $3.90, 20.00%   48. $3.50, 20.00%

49. $M = C \times C\%$ or $R = C + M$
    $M = \$9.50 \times .46$ $R = 100\%C + 46\%C$
    $M = \$4.37$ $R = 146\%C$
    $R = C + M$ $R = 1.46 \times \$9.50$
    $R = \$9.50 + \$4.37$ $R = \$13.87$
    $R = \$13.87$

50. $M = C \times C\%$ or $R = C + M$
    $M = \$67.50 \times .45$ $R = 100\%C + 45\%C$
    $M = \$30.38$ $R = 145\%C$
    $R = C + M$ $R = 1.45 \times \$67.50$
    $R = \$67.50 + \$30.38$ $R = \$97.88$
    $R = \$97.88$

51. $\$126 \div 12 = \$10.50$ 52. $R\% = M/R = \$22.15/\$49.95 = 44.34\%$
    $R - C = M$
    $\$14.99 - \$10.50 = M$
    $\$4.49 = M$
    $C\% = M/C = \$4.49/\$10.50 = 42.76\%$

53. $R = C + M$ 54. $R = C + M$
    $100\%R = C + 31.5\%R$ $100\%R = C + 40\%R$
    $68.5\%R = C$ $60\%R = C$
    $R = \$3.75/.685 = \$5.47$ $R = C/60\% = \$12/.60 = \$20$

55. $R = C + M$ 56. $R = C + M$
    $R = 100\%C + 25\%C$ $R = 100\%C + 30\%C$
    $R = 125\%C$ $R = 130\%C$
    $R/125\% = C$ $R/130\% = C$
    $\$38/1.25 = C$ $\$18/1.3 = \$13.85$
    $\$30.40 = C$

57. $M = R \times R\%$ or $R = C + M$
    $M = \$35 \times .2$ $100\%R = C + 20\%R$
    $M = \$7$ $80\%R = C$
    $R - M = C$ $.8 \times \$35 = C$
    $35 - 7 = C$ $\$28 = C$
    $\$28 = C$

22

58. $\underline{M} = \underline{R} \times \underline{R\%}$ or $\underline{R} = \underline{C} + \underline{M}$
     $\underline{M} = \$42 \times .38$ $\overline{100\%R} = \underline{C} + 38\%R$
     $\underline{M} = \$15.96$ $62\%R = \underline{C}$
     $\underline{R} - \underline{M} = \underline{C}$ $\underline{C} = 62\%\underline{R} = .62 \times \$42 = \$26.04$
     $\overline{\$42.00} - 15.96 = \underline{C}$
     $\$26.04 = \underline{C}$

59. $\underline{R} - \underline{C} = \underline{M}$ 60. $\underline{R} - \underline{C} = \underline{M}$
     $\$8 - \$4.50 = \underline{M}$ $\$9 - \$3 = \underline{M}$
     $\$3.50 = \underline{M}$ $\$6 = \underline{M}$
     $\underline{R\%} = \underline{M}/\underline{R} = \$3.50/\$8.00 = 43.75\%$ $\underline{C\%} = \underline{M}/\underline{C} = \$6/\$3 = 2.00 = 200\%$

61. $\underline{R} = \underline{C} + \underline{M}$ 62. $\underline{R} = \underline{C} + \underline{M}$
     $\overline{100\%R} = \underline{C} + 35\%\underline{R}$ $\overline{100\%R} = \underline{C} + 38\%\underline{R}$
     $65\%\underline{R} = \underline{C}$ $72\%\underline{R} = \underline{C}$
     $\underline{R} = \underline{C}/65\% = \$10/.65 = \$15.38$ $\underline{R} = \underline{C}/72\% = \$42.50/.72 = \$59.03$

<u>Learning Unit 5.2</u>

<u>Markon on Seasonal</u>

<u>or Perishable Goods</u>

1. 50 pounds at $1.06 = $53.00 cost; 40% markon = $21.20
    20% spoilage = 10 pounds; therefore, we must sell 40 pounds for a
    total of $74.20 or $1.86 per pound (rounded).

2. 125 pounds at $1.58 = $197.50 cost; 40% markon = $79.00
    10% spoilage = 12 1/2 pounds; therefore, we must sell 112 1/2 pounds
    for a total of $276.50 or $2.46 per pound (rounded).

3. 150 pounds at $1.28 = $192.00 cost; 40% markon = $76.80
    15% spoilage = 22.5 pounds; therefore, we must sell 127 1/2 pounds for
    a total of $268.80 or $2.11 per pound (rounded).

4. 500 pounds at $1.87 = $935.00 cost; 40% markon = $374.00
    30% spoilage = 150 pounds; therefore, we must sell 350 pounds for a
    total of $1,309.00 or $3.74 per pound.

5. 30 x $42 = $1,260 cost + 40% markon of $504 = $1,764
    90% (or 27 pair) will sell at full price and 10% (or 3 pair) will sell
    at 1/2 of full price. Let $\underline{P}$ = selling price:
    $27\underline{P} + 3(\underline{P}/2) = \$1,764$
        $28\ 1/2\underline{P} = \$1,764$
            $\underline{P} = \$1,764/28.5;\ \underline{P} = \$61.89$ per pair

6. 75 x $68 = $5,100 cost + 40% markon of $2,040 = $7,140
    85% (or 64 pair) will sell at full price and 15% (or 11 pair) will
    sell at 1/2 of full price. Let $\underline{P}$ = selling price:
    $64\underline{P} + 11(\underline{P}/2) = \$7,140$
        $69\ 1/2\underline{P} = \$7,140$
            $\underline{P} = \$7,140/69.5;\ \underline{P} = \$102.73$ per pair

7. 90 x $99 = $8,910 cost + 40% markon of $3,564 = $12,474
    65% (or 59 pair) will sell at full price and 35% (or 31 pair) will
    sell at 1/2 of full price. Let $\underline{P}$ = selling price:
    $59\underline{P} + 31(\underline{P}/2) = \$12,474$
        $74\ 1/2\underline{P} = \$12,474$
            $\underline{P} = \$12,474/74.5;\ \underline{P} = \$167.44$ per pair

8. 175 x $15 = $2,625.00 cost + 40% markon of $1,050.00 = $3,675.00
    95% (or 166 pair) will sell at full price and 5% (or 9 pair) will sell
    at 9/10 of full price. Let $\underline{P}$ = selling price:
    $166\underline{P} + 9(9\underline{P}/10) = \$3,675$
    $\qquad\qquad 174.1\underline{P} = \$3,675$
    $\qquad\qquad\qquad \underline{P} = \$3,675/174.1;\ \underline{P} = \$21.11$ per pair

9. Cost = 10 x $4 = $40
    Total pounds = 400 (10 boxes x 40 lbs.)
    $\underline{M} = \underline{C}$ x $\underline{C}\%$ $\qquad$ $\underline{R} = \underline{C} + \underline{M}$
    $\underline{M} = \$40$ x $.25$ $\qquad$ $\underline{R} = \$40 + \$10$
    $\underline{M} = \$10$ $\qquad\qquad$ $\underline{R} = \$50$
    10% or 40 pounds will not be sold; therefore, 360 pounds must sell
    for $50.
    Price per pound = $50/360 = $.14 (rounded to whole cents)

10. $\underline{M} = \underline{C}$ x $\underline{C}\%$ $\qquad$ $\underline{R} = \underline{C} + \underline{M}$
    $\underline{M} = \$60$ x $.40$ $\qquad$ $\underline{R} = \$60 + \$24$
    $\underline{M} = \$24$ $\qquad\qquad$ $\underline{R} = \$84$
    8% or 24 pounds will not be sold; therefore, 276 pounds must sell
    for $84.
    Price per pound = $84/276 = $.3043 = $.30*
    (*Most stores would probably round to the higher cent = $.31.)

11. $\underline{R} = \underline{C} + \underline{M}$ $\qquad\qquad$ Cost = 50 x $3.50 = $175
    $100\%\underline{R} = \underline{C} + 30\%\underline{R}$
    $70\%\underline{R} = \underline{C}$
    $\underline{R} = \underline{C}/70\% = \$175/.7 = \$250$
    10% or 5 plants are not expected to sell; therefore, 45 plants must
    sell for $250.
    Price per plant = $250/45 = $5.56

12. $\underline{R} = \underline{C} + \underline{M}$
    $100\%\underline{R} = \underline{C} + 40\%\underline{M}$
    $60\%\underline{R} = \underline{C}$
    $\underline{R} = \underline{C}/60\% = \$10/.6 = \$16.67$
    2 dozen are not expected to be sold; therefore, 16 dozen donuts must
    sell for $16.67.
    Price per dozen = $16.67/16 = $1.04
    Price per donut = Price per dozen/12 = $1.04/12 = $.0867 = $.09

13. $\underline{R} = \underline{C} + \underline{M}$ $\qquad\quad$ or $\quad$ Cost = $6 x 60 = $360
    $\underline{R} = 100\%\underline{C} + 50\%\underline{C}$ $\qquad$ $\underline{R} = \underline{C} + \underline{M}$
    $\underline{R} = 150\%\underline{C}$ $\qquad\qquad$ $\underline{R} = 100\%\underline{C} + 50\%\underline{C}$
    $\underline{R} = 1.50$ x $\$6 = \$9$ $\qquad$ $\underline{R} = 150\%\underline{C}$
    60 ties x $9 = $540 $\qquad$ $\underline{R} = 1.5$ x $\$360 = \$540$
    15% or 9 ties will be sold at 1/2 price and 51 will be sold at full
    price.
    $51\underline{p} + 9 . \underline{p}/2 = \$540$
    $51\underline{p} + 4.5\underline{p} = \$540$
    $55.5\underline{p} = \$540$
    $\underline{p} = \$540/55.5 = \$9.729 = \$9.73$

14. Cost = 2,000 x $.30 = $600
    $\underline{R} = \underline{C} + \underline{M}$
    $100\%\underline{R} = \underline{C} + 40\%\underline{R}$
    $60\%\underline{R} = \underline{C}$
    $\underline{R} = \underline{C}/.60 = \$600/.60 = \$1,000$

20% or 400 bags will be sold for $.10 each; therefore, $40 of the
$1,000 will come from the sale of 400 bags and the remaining $960 must
come from the sale of 1,600 bags.
Price per bag = $960/1,600 = $.60

15. $\underline{R}$ = $\underline{C}$ + $\underline{M}$
$\underline{C}$ = (50 lbs. x $1.00) + ($5.25) = $55.25
$\underline{M}$ = 100%C or $55.25
$\underline{R}$ = $55.25 + $55.25 = $110.50
Joe needs to make $110.50 from the sale of french fries. He will sell
only 46 pounds (50 - 4), or 184 servings (46 x 4 per pound); therefore,
each serving will cost $.60.

$$\frac{\$ \quad .6005}{184)\$110.5000} = \$.60/\text{serving (rounded to the nearest penny)}$$

16. 60 + 10% = 60 + 6 = 66 pizzas
$\underline{C}$ = 66 pizzas x $1.90 = $125.40
$\underline{M}$ = 60%C = .6 x $125.40 = $75.24
$\underline{R}$ = $\underline{C}$ + $\underline{M}$
$\underline{R}$ = $125.40 + $75.24 = $200.64
Anthony must collect $200.64 from 50 people.

$$\frac{\$ \quad 4.01}{50)\$200.64}$$

$4.01 is the correct answer to the nearest penny; however, the price
will probably be $3.99.

Learning Unit 5.3

Markup and Markdown

1. Markup = $5 ($15 - 10)
    Difference = Amount of markup = $5
2. $5; 25%   3. $6; 16 2/3%   4. $6; 33 1/3%
5. $20; 50%   6. $6; 25%   7. $4; 40%
8. $2; 12 1/2%   9. $12; 37 1/2%   10. $.20; 40%
11. $.05; .05/.20 = 1/4 = 25% markdown   12. $10; 50%
13. $4; 25%   14. $3; 33 1/3%   15. $5; 100%
16. $1; 12 1/2%   17. $7; 50%   18. $3; 20%
19. $2; 40%   20. $.04; 16 2/3%

21. $\underline{R}$ = P/$\underline{B}$
      50% = 50% $\underline{B}$/$45 - 50%B

$$\tfrac{1}{2} = \frac{\frac{1}{2}B}{\$45 - \frac{1}{2}B}$$

    $2(\tfrac{1}{2}B)$ = $45 - $\tfrac{1}{2}B$
    3/2B = $45

$$\underline{B} = \frac{\$45}{3/2}$$

    $\underline{B}$ = $45/1 x 2/3
    $\underline{B}$ = $30

22. $9   23. $10   24. $20

25. $\underline{R} = \underline{P}/\underline{B}$

$$33\ 1/3\% = \frac{33\ 1/3\%\underline{B}}{\$6 + 33\ 1/3\%\underline{B}}$$

$$1/3 = \frac{1/3\underline{B}}{\$6 + 1/3\underline{B}}$$

$$\underline{B} = \$6 + 1/3\ \underline{B}$$

$$2/3\ \underline{B} = \$6$$

$$\underline{B} = \frac{6}{2/3} = \frac{\$6}{1} \times \frac{3}{2} = \$9$$

26. $20   27. $50   28. $.20

29. $40 - $25 = $15   30. $1,500; 30% markup
      15/40 = 3/8 = 37 1/2% markup

31. $125 - $75 = $50   32. $3; 60% markdown
      $50/$75 = 2/3 = 66 2/3% markdown

33. $\underline{R} = \underline{P}/\underline{B}$
      $28\% = 28\%\underline{B}/\$124.95 - 28\%\underline{B}$
      $\underline{B} = \$97.62$ sale price
      $\$124.95 - 97.62 = \$27.33$ dollar markdown

34. $29.96   35. $71.43   36. $43.75

Chapter 5
Self-Evaluation

1. $\underline{R} = \$30 + \$15;\ \underline{R} = \$45$
2. $\underline{C} = \$40 - \$12;\ \underline{C} = \$28$
3. $\underline{R} = 130\%\underline{C};\ \underline{R} = 1.3 \times \$10;\ \underline{R} = \$13$
4. $\$18 = 150\%\underline{C};\ \$18/1.5 = \underline{C};\ \$12 = \underline{C}$
5. $60\%\underline{R} = \$20;\ \underline{R} = \$20/.6;\ \underline{R} = \$33.33$
6. $\underline{M} = 25\%\underline{C};\ \$10 = 25\%\underline{C};\ \$10/.25 = \underline{C};\ \$40 = \underline{C}.\ \ \underline{R} = \underline{C} + \underline{M}:\ \underline{R} = \$40 + \$10;$
     $\underline{R} = \$50$
7.   300 lbs. x $.20 = $60 cost + $30 (= 50% of cost) = $90 (total retail
     price)
     300 - 90 lbs. (30% not sold) = 210 lbs.
     $90/210 = $.43 per lb.
8. $48\underline{R} + 32 \times 75\%\underline{R} = \$260;\ 48\underline{R} + 24\underline{R} = \$260;\ 72\underline{R} = \$260;\ \underline{R} = \$260/72;$
     $\underline{R} = \$3.61$
9. $\underline{M} = \underline{NRP} - \underline{ORP};\ \underline{m} = \$25 - \$20;\ \underline{m} = \$5.\ \ \%\underline{m} = \$5/\underline{NRP} = \$5/25 = 1/5 = 20\%$
10. $\underline{m} = \underline{ORP} - \underline{NRP};\ \underline{m} = \$20 - \$15;\ \underline{m} = \$5.\ \ \%\underline{m} = 5/15 = 1/3 = 33\ 1/3\%$

Chapter 6

Payroll Accounting

A.   Purpose

This chapter explains some of the compensation methods used in business as
well as the various types of payroll deductions.

B.   Comments

 1. Federal withholding tax tables and F.I.C.A. tax amounts change regu-
     larly; therefore, the tables, rates, and maximum taxable amounts in-
     cluded in this chapter are as current as possible. Current Circular E
     publications (available from IRS office) may be consulted for exact
     updating.
 2. The compensation methods discussed in this chapter are merely repre-
     sentative and do not cover all possible ways of being paid for work
     performed.

C.   Solutions

Learning Unit 6.1

Compensation Methods

 1. $15,000/12 = $1,250   2. $1,520.00   3. $340.00
 4. $830.77   5. $701.54   6. $7.20 x 40 = $288.00
                               $10.80 x 2 = $21.60
                               $288.00 + $21.60 = $309.60

 7. $312.80   8. $173.38   9. $282.00

10. $284.90   11. $2.80 x 40 = $112.00   12. $224.00
                    $4.00 x 32 = $128.00
                    $112.00 + $128.00 = $240

13. $204.80   14. $276.00   15. $94.40
16. $3,600 x .12 = $432.00   17. $351.00   18. $1,010.00
19. $1,213.60   20. $646.50   21. $1,396.88

22. $15,500/26 = $596.15   23. $7.48 x 40 = $299.20
                                   $11.22 x 2 = $22.44
                                   $299.20 + $22.44 = $321.64

24. $2.95 x 40 = $118.00   25. $72,000 - $45,000 = $27,000
    $3,200 x .005 = $16.00 $45,000 x .02 = $900.00
    $118.00 + $16.00 = $134.00 $27,000 x .025 = $675.00
                                     $900.00 + $675.00 = $1,575.00

26. $160/40 = $4/hour reg. rate
    $4 x 1 1/2 = $6/hour overtime rate
    40 x $4 = $160 regular pay
    7 x $6 = $42 overtime pay
    $160 + $42 = $202 total weekly pay

27. $200/35 = $5.71/hour regular rate
    $5.71 x 1 1/2 = $8.57/hour overtime rate
    35 x $5.71 = $199.85 (due to rounding) but she will receive $200
    7 x $8.57 = $59.99
    $200 + $59.99 = $259.99 total weekly pay

28. 42.5 total hours = 38 regular hours + 4.5 overtime hours
     1.5 x $4.50 = $6.75/hour overtime rate
     38 x $4.50 = $171.00 regular pay
     4.5 x $6.75 = $30.38 overtime pay
    42.5 hours = $201.38 gross pay

29. 47.5 total hours = 40 regular hours + 7.5 overtime hours
     1.5 x $7.80 = $11.70/hour overtime rate
     40 x $7.80 = $312.00 regular pay
     7.5 x $11.70 = $87.75 overtime pay
    47.5 hours = $399.75 gross pay

30. $750,000.00 gross sales
    -150,000.00 discounts given
    - 7,855.50 merchandise returned

    $592,144.50 net sales x .005 = $2,960.72 gross pay

Learning Unit 6.2

Payroll Deductions

1. $26.90   2. $24.90   3. $55.50
4. $37.00   5. $16.80   6. $58.10
7. $304.00 x .0613 = $18.64   8. $11.03
9. $25.32   10. $13.24   11. $10.30   12. $19.13

	Regular Pay	Overtime Pay	Gross Pay	Deductions						Net Pay
				FIT	FICA	HI	CU	RP	Total	
13.	300.00	45.00	345.00	39.30	21.15	28.43			88.88	256.12
14.	330.00	-0-	330.00	45.50	20.23		10.00		75.73	254.27
15.	290.00	-0-	290.00	52.10	17.78			25.00	94.88	195.12
16.	270.00	60.75	330.75	54.70	20.27	28.43			103.40	227.35
17.	256.00	-0-	256.00	41.60	15.69	18.60			75.89	180.11
18.	360.00	-0-	360.00	39.40	22.07		10.00	15.00	86.47	273.53
19.	290.00	32.63	322.63	39.10	19.78	28.43			87.31	235.32
20.	265.00	-0-	265.00	44.20	16.24		20.00		80.44	184.56
21.	287.00	-0-	287.00	54.80	17.59	18.60			90.99	196.01
	2,648.00	138.38	2,786.38	410.70	170.80	122.49	40.00	40.00	783.99	2,002.39

	Regular Pay	Overtime Pay	Gross Pay	Deductions						Net Pay
				FIT	FICA	HI	CU	RP	Total	
22.	300.00	-0-	300.00	30.90	18.39	28.43			77.72	222.28
23.	330.00	61.88	391.88	59.90	24.02		10.00		93.92	297.96
24.	315.00	-0-	315.00	41.10	19.31			25.00	85.41	229.59
25.	284.00	42.60	326.60	52.30	20.02	28.43			100.75	225.85
26.	275.00	-0-	275.00	46.80	16.86				63.66	211.34
27.	301.55	-0-	301.55	55.10	18.49	18.60			92.19	209.36
28.	380.00	-0-	380.00	43.70	23.29			15.00	81.99	298.01
29.	316.00	-0-	316.00	33.00	19.37	28.43			80.80	235.20
30.	265.00	-0-	265.00	44.20	16.24		20.00		80.44	184.56
	2,766.55	104.48	2,871.03	407.00	175.99	103.89	30.00	40.00	756.88	2,114.15

31. $30.00   32. $54.29   33. $30.19   34. $43.13
35. $56.70   36. $247.82   37. $85.84   38. $28.95

39. $2,350 x 12 = $28,200 yearly salary
    $28,200/26 = $1,084.62 biweekly salary
    $1,084.62 x .0613 = $66.49 FICA tax

40. $5.80 x 40 = $232
    Tax = $24.60

41. $18,000/52 = $346.15 weekly salary
    $346.15 x .0613 = $21.22 FICA tax
    $21.22 + $43.00 + $38.00 + $43.30 = $145.52 total deductions
    $346.15 - $145.52 = $200.63 net pay

42. $22,100/52 = $425.00 weekly salary
    $425 x .0613 = $26.05 FICA tax
    $26.05 + $27.00 + $33.00 + $73.20 = $159.25 total deductions
    $425.00 - $159.25 = $265.75 net pay

43. $2,875.00 gross pay
    - 333.32 ($83.33 monthly withholding allowance x 4)
    $2,541.68 taxable income for federal income tax

    $516.64 plus 37% of the excess over $2,408 ($49.46) =
    $566.10 federal income tax using percentage method

    $ 2,875.00
    +24,300.00
    $27,175.00 total earnings including this check
    -25,900.00 maximum taxable for FICA
    $ 1,275.00 nontaxable for FICA

    $2,875 - $1,275 = $1,600 taxable for FICA
    $1,600 x .0613 = $98.08 FICA tax

    $2,875.00 gross pay   *$566.10 federal income tax
    - 664.18*total tax   + 98.08 FICA
    $2,210.82 net pay $664.18 total tax deductions

44. $256.80

45. federal income tax $238.40
    FICA ($1525 x .0613)   93.48
    credit union   50.00
    insurance   38.50
      total deductions $420.38

    $1,525 - $420.38 = $1,104.62 net pay

46. $30,000/12 = $2,500/month
    Jan.-Oct. = 10 months x $2,500 = $25,000
         Nov. = 1 month x $2,500 =   2,500
                                     $27,500
                                     -25,900 maximum taxable for FICA
                                     $ 1,600 nontaxable for FICA

    Nov. check $2,500 - $1,600 = $900 taxable for FICA

```
        FICA = $900 x .0613 = $ 55.17
        Federal tax =           519.80
          Total tax            $574.97

        $2,500 - $574.97 = $1,925.03 net pay
```

47.   I. $24,700 year-to-date earnings
             + 2,650 this month's salary
             $27,350
             -25,900 maximum taxable for FICA
             $ 1,450 nontaxable for FICA

             $ 2,650 monthly income
              -1,450 nontaxable for FICA
             $ 1,200 taxable for FICA

       II. $2,650 taxable for federal income tax (no exemptions)
             From Table 6.7, tax = $516.64 + 37% over $2,408

Income	Fed. income tax
$2,408	$516.64
242 x .37 =	89.54
$2,650	$606.18

       III. gross salary $2,650.00 ------------------- $2,650.00
             Fed. income tax   606.18
             FICA ($1,200 x .0613)   73.56 total deductions-   717.24
             Insurance   37.50   net pay- $1,932.76

48.   I. $18,800/52 weeks = $361.54 per week

       II. $19.23 weekly exemption
             x   4
             $76.92 nontaxable
             $361.54 gross pay
             - 76.92 nontaxable
             $284.62 taxable income

             Using Table 6.6b, federal income tax =
             $27.09 + 21% of the excess over $210 (.21 x $74.62) = $42.76

       III. gross pay $361.54/week
             federal income tax $ 42.76
             FICA ($361.54 x .0613)   22.16
             insurance   15.00
             union dues   5.00
             credit union   25.00
               total deductions $109.92   -109.92
                                             $251.62 net pay

Chapter 6
Self-Evaluation

1. $22,620/12 = $1,885
2. $1,600 x 12 = $19,200 annual/26 = $738.46
3. $7.80 x 40 = $312.00

4. $8.25 x 40 = $330.00
    $12.375 x 2 = <u> 24.75</u>   (8.75 x 1.5 = $12.375)
                  $354.75

5. $2.65 x 40 = $106
    $3.00 x 50 = <u> 150</u>
                 $256

6. $10,000 x .05 = $500.00
     5,700 x .08 = <u> 456.00</u>
                   $956.00

7. $32,000/12 = $2,666.67 per month salary
    5 x $83.33 = <u> 416.65</u> exempt
                 $2,250.02 taxable earnings

    deductions: FICA $163.47   *$2,250.02   tax from table
                 *fed. tax   466.09   <u>-1,967.00</u> $375.52
                 insurance   57.00 $ 283.02 x 32% =   <u> 90.57</u>
                 retirement   <u> 70.00</u> $466.09
                               $756.56

    $2,666.67 - $756.56 = $1,910.11 net pay

8. $1,365 x 12 = $16,380/52 = $315 per week
    (a) Federal income tax = $58.10 from table
    (b) FICA = .0613 x $315 = $19.31

9. Maximum FICA wages = $25,900
                         <u>-24,900</u>
                         $ 1,000 taxable x .0613 = $61.30

Chapter 7

Depreciation

A.   Purpose

This chapter explains the four principal methods of computing depreciation:
(1) straight-line, (2) units-of-production, (3) sum-of-the-years-digits,
and (4) declining balance. After studying this chapter, the student should
understand the process of depreciation: why plant assets are depreciated;
when depreciation is computed; what factors are involved in determining the
amount of depreciation to recognize during an accounting period; how the
total cost of a plant asset is determined; how depreciation is computed
under each of the four methods; and how the book value of a plant asset is
determined.

B.   Comments

1.   The concept of depreciation and the methods used to compute deprecia-
     tion should be thoroughly explained to ensure the student's under-
     standing.
2.   Special emphasis should be given the fact that, in computing deprecia-
     tion using a declining-balance method, the residual value is not sub-
     tracted from the cost of an asset as it is in the other methods.
3.   It should also be emphasized that, like the other depreciation methods,
     the process of depreciating an asset ends when the book value is equal
     to the estimated residual value. (The book value is never reduced be-
     low the residual value when using the depreciation methods explained
     in this chapter.)

C.   Solutions

Learning Unit 7.1

Depreciation Based on

Years of Service Life

1. $4,300 - $300 = $4,000 amount to be depreciated
     100% ÷ 4 = 25% = .25 straight-line depreciation rate
     $4,000 x .25 = $1,000 annual depreciation

2.   .$10,000; $2,000   3. $18,500; $2,312.50   4. $19,575; $3,915
5. $21,789; $3,631.50   6. $32,274; $4,610.57
7.   September + October + November + December = 4 months
8.   4 months   9.   11 months   10.   1 month
11. 10 months   12.   11 months

13. $10,300 - $700 = $9,600 amount to be depreciated
     100% ÷ 8 = 12.5% = .125 annual straight-line depreciation rate
     $9,600 x .125 = $1,200 annual straight-line depreciation
     October + November + December = 3 months in the first fiscal year
     $1,200 x 3/12 = $300 depreciation for the first fiscal year

14. $2,000   15. $1,047.62   16. $3,501
17. $1,263.64   18. $3,893.78

19.

Year	Cost	Depreciation Expense	Accumulated Depreciation	Book Value
0	$8,300	$ -0-	$ -0-	$8,300
1	8,300	1,500	1,500	6,800
2	8,300	1,500	3,000	5,300
3	8,300	1,500	4,500	3,800
4	8,300	1,500	6,000	2,300
5	8,300	1,500	7,500	800

20. $7,752 - $3,300 = $4,452 amount to be depreciated
     100% ÷ 3 = .3333333 or 1/3 annual straight-line depreciation rate
     $4,452 x 1/3 = $1,484 annual straight-line depreciation

21. $1,576 - $350 = $1,226 amount to be depreciated
     100% ÷ 10 = .1 annual straight-line depreciation rate
     $1,226 x .1 = $122.60 annual straight-line depreciation

22. $473 - $100 = $373 book value

23. $865 - $65 = $800 amount to be depreciated
     100% ÷ 5 = .2 annual straight-line depreciation rate
     $800 x .2 = $160 annual straight-line depreciation

24. $320 - $192 = $128 accumulated depreciation

25. $8,654 x .05 = $432.70 sales tax
     $8,654 + $432.70 + $352 + $36 = $9,474.70 total cost

26. $9,895 - $3,500 = $6,395 amount to be depreciated
    100% ÷ 4 = .25 annual straight-line depreciation rate
    $6,395 x .25 = $1,598.75 annual straight-line depreciation
    $1,598.75 x 2 = $3,197.50 depreciation first two years
    $9,895 - $3,197.50 = $6,697.50 book value end 2nd year

27. $919 - $100 = $819 amount to be depreciated
    100% ÷ 10 = .1 annual straight-line depreciation rate
    $819 x .1 = $81.90 annual straight-line depreciation
    October through December = 3 months in 1st fiscal year
    $81.90 x 3/12 = $20.475 = $20.48 first year depreciation
    $81.90 + $20.48 = $102.38 depreciation 1st and 2nd years
    $919 - $102.38 = $816.62 book value end 2nd year

28.

Year	Cost	Depreciation Expense	Accumulated Depreciation	Book Value
0	$16,800	$ -0-	$ -0-	$16,800
1	16,800	2,600	2,600	14,200
2	16,800	2,600	5,200	11,600
3	16,800	2,600	7,800	9,000
4	16,800	2,600	10,400	6,400
5	16,800	2,600	13,000	3,800
6	16,800	2,600	15,600	1,200

Learning Unit 7.2

Depreciation Base on

Productive Capacity

1. $6,450 - $450 = $6,000   2. $41,400; $5.52; $3,908.16
    $6,000/10,000 = $.60
    1,342 x $.60 = $805.20   3. $63,000; $1.26; $6,737.22

4. $58,050; $.43; $3,827.43   5. $182,245; $2.87; $5,866.28

6. $52,000; $.16; $7,400   7. $57,000 - $7,000 = $50,000
                                   $50,000 ÷ 100,000 = $.50
8. $2,975; $.035; $602.11   2,166 x $.50 = $1,083

9. $157,500; $.63; $24,640.56 10. $3,290; $.0365555; $317.08

11. $8,625; $.069; $1,815.18   12. $9,860; $.058; $108.17

13. $450,000 - $150,000 = $300,000
    $300,000 ÷ 10,000 = $30 per hour
    $30 x 520 = $15,600 depreciation

14. $395,250 ÷ 75,000 = $5.27 per unit
    $5.27 x 10,500 = $55,335 depreciation

15. (a) $6,795 - $700 = $6,095
        $6,095 ÷ 5 = $1,219
        $1,219 x 3/12 = $304.75 straight-line
    (b) $6,095 ÷ 100,000 = $.061
        $.06095 x 7,200 = $438.84 units-of-production

16. (a) $9,720/4 = $2,430
         $2,430 x 10/12 = $2,025 straight-line
     (b) $9,720/13,500 = $.72
         $.72 x 4,108 = $2,957.76 units-of-production

Learning Unit 7.3

Accelerated Depreciation--

Sum-of-the-Years-Digits Method

1. $S = \underline{N}(\underline{N} + 1)/2 = 3(3 + 1)/2 = 12/2 = 6$
2. $\underline{10}$ 3. 21   4. 36   5. 45
6. 78   7. 120   8. 325

9. $S = \underline{N}(\underline{N} + 1)/2 = 8(8 + 1)/2 = 72/2 = 36$
    $1,752 - $100 = $1,652
    $1,652 x 8/36 = $367.11
    $1,752 - $367.11 = $1,384.89

10. $S = \underline{N}(\underline{N} + 1)/2 = 4(4 + 1)/2 = 20/2 = 10$
    $7,560 - $1,300 = $6,260
    $6,260 x 4/10 = $2,504
    $7,560 - $2,504 = $5,056

11. $S = \underline{N}(\underline{N} + 1)/2 = 5(5 + 1)/2 = 30/2 = 15$
    $852 - $150 = $702
    $702 x 5/15 = $234
    $852 - $234 = $618

12. $S = \underline{N}(\underline{N} + 1)/2 = 7(7 + 1)/2 = 56/2 = 28$
    $47,250 - $12,000 = $35,250
    $35,250 x 7/28 = $8,812.50
    $47,250 - $8,812.50 = $38,437.50

13. $9,474.70 - $1,000 = $8,474.70 amount to be depreciated

Year	Cost	Depreciation Fraction	Depreciation Expense	Accumulated Depreciation	Book Value
0	$9,474.70		$ -0-	$ -0-	$9,474.70
1	9,474.70	4/10	3,389.88	3,389.88	6,084.82
2	9,474.70	3/10	2,542.41	5,932.29	3,542.41
3	9,474.70	2/10	1,694.94	7,627.23	1,847.47
4	9,474.70	1/10	847.47	8,474.70	1,000.00

14. $8,752 - $3,300 = $5,452 amount to be depreciated

Year	Cost	Depreciation Fraction	Depreciation Expense	Accumulated Depreciation	Book Value
0	$8,752		$ -0-	$ -0-	$8,752.00
1	8,752	3/6	2,726.00	2,726.00	6,026.00
2	8,752	2/6	1,817.33	4,543.33	4,208.67
3	8,752	1/6	908.67	5,452.00	3,300.00

15. $71,340 - $23,000 = $48,340 amount to be depreciated

Year	Cost	Depreciation Fraction	Depreciation Expense	Accumulated Depreciation	Book Value
0	$71,340		$ -0-	$ -0-	$71,340.00
1	71,340	5/15	16,113.33	16,113.33	55,226.67
2	71,340	4/15	12,890.67	29,004.00	42,336.00
3	71,340	3/15	9,668.00	38,672.00	32,668.00
4	71,340	2/15	6,445.33	45,117.33	26,222.67
5	71,340	1/15	3,222.67	48,340.00	23,000.00

16. $24,600 - $4,000 = $20,600

Year	Cost	Depreciation Fraction	Depreciation Expense	Accumulated Depreciation	Book Value
0	$24,600		$ -0-	$ -0-	$24,600.00
1	24,600	8/36	4,577.78	4,577.78	20,022.22
2	24,600	7/36	4,005.56	8,583.34	16,016.66
3	24,600	6/36	3,433.33	12,016.67	12,583.33
4	24,600	5/36	2,861.11	14,877.78	9,722.22
5	24,600	4/36	2,288.89	17,166.67	7,433.33
6	24,600	3/36	1,716.67	18,883.34	5,716.66
7	24,600	2/36	1,144.44	20,027.78	4,572.22
8	24,600	1/36	572.22	20,600.00	4,000.00

Learning Unit 7.4

Accelerated Depreciation:

Double-Declining-Balance Method

1. (100% ÷ 4) x 2 = 50%   2. 25%
3. 33 1/3%   4. 40%   5. 20%
6. 13 1/3%   7. 8%   8. 16 2/3%

9. (100% ÷ 8) x 2 = 25%   10. (100% ÷ 4) x 2 = 50%
    $1,752 x .25 = $438 $7,560 x .5 = $3,780
    $1,752 - $438 = $1,314 $7,560 - $3,780 = $3,780

11. (100% ÷ 5) x 2 = 40%   12. (100% ÷ 7) x 2 = 28.57142%
     $852 x .4 = $340.80 $47,250 x .2857142 = $13,500
     $852 - $340.80 = $511.20 $47,250 - $13,500 = $33,750

13. $9,474.70 - $1,000 = $8,474.70 amount to be depreciated

Year	Cost	Depreciation Rate	Depreciation Expense	Accumulated Depreciation	Book Value
0	$9,474.70		$ -0-	$ -0-	$9,474.70
1	9,474.70	.5	4,737.35	4,737.35	4,737.35
2	9,474.70	.5	2,368.68	7,106.03	2,368.68
3	9,474.70	.5	1,184.34	8,290.37	1,184.34
4	9,474.70	.5	184.34	8,474.70	1,000.00

14. $8,752 - $3,300 = $5,452 amount to be depreciated

Year	Cost	Depreciation Rate	Depreciation Expense	Accumulated Depreciation	Book Value
0	$8,752		$ -0-	$ -0-	$8,752.00
1	8,752	2/3	5,452.00	5,452.00	3,300.00
2	8,752	2/3	-0-	5,452.00	3,300.00
3	8,752	2/3	-0-	5,452.00	3,300.00

15. $71,340 - $23,000 = $48,340 amount to be depreciated

Year	Cost	Depreciation Rate	Depreciation Expense	Accumulated Depreciation	Book Value
0	$71,340		$ -0-	$ -0-	$71,340.00
1	71,340	.4	28,536.00	28,536.00	42,804.00
2	71,340	.4	17,121.60	45,657.60	25,682.40
3	71,340	4	2,682.40	48,340.00	23,000.00
4	71,340	.4	-0-	48,340.00	23,000.00
5	71,340	.4	-0-	48,340.00	23,000.00

16. $24,600 - $4,000 = $20,600 amount to be depreciated

Year	Cost	Depreciation Rate	Depreciation Expense	Accumulated Depreciation	Book Value
0	$24,600		$ -0-	$ -0-	$24,600.00
1	24,600	.25	6,150.00	6,150.00	18,450.00
2	24,600	.25	4,612.50	10,762.50	13,837.50
3	24,600	.25	3,459.38	14,221.88	10,378.12
4	24,600	.25	2,594.53	16,816.41	7,783.59
5	24,600	.25	1,945.90	18,762.31	5,837.69
6	24,600	.25	1,459.42	20,221.73	4,378.27
7	24,600	.25	378.27	20,600.00	4,000.00
8	24,600	.25	-0-	20,600.00	4,000.00

Chapter 7
Self-Evaluation

1. $5,545 - $800 = $4,745 amount to be depreciated
   100%/8 = .125 annual straight-line depreciation rate
   $4,745 x .125 = $593.125 = $593.13 annual depreciation

2. $16,800 - $1,800 = $15,000 amount to be depreciated
   $15,000/30,000 = $.50 depreciation rate per machine hour
   2,320 x $.50 = $1,160 depreciation

3. $5,545 - $800 = $4,745 amount to be depreciated
   $S = \underline{N(N + 1)/2} = 8(8 + 1)/2 = 72/2 = 36$ sum-of-the-years-digits
   $4,745 x 8/36 = $1,054.44 first-year depreciation

4. (100%/8) x 2 = .25 double-declining-balance depreciation rate
   $5,545 x .25 = $1,386.25 first-year depreciation

5. $319 - $50 = $269 amount to be depreciated
   100%/10 = .1 annual straight-line depreciation rate
   $269 x .1 = $26.90 annual depreciation
   October through December = 3 months during 1st fiscal year
   $26.90 x 3/12 = $6.725 = $6.73 depreciation 1st year

Chapter 8

Inventory

A. Purpose

Most businesses maintain a stock of supplies, tools, equipment, products for
sale, and other types of assets that are subject to some type of periodic
count. In a broad sense, all resources of a business could be considered
inventory. This chapter describes the methods used by businesses for determining the cost and valuation of inventory items.

B. Comments

 1. Adequate and accurate records must be maintained in order to utilize
     any of the four inventory valuation methods.
 2. Different methods are best under different circumstances, e.g., weighted
     average cost is best when the unit cost is very low and does not jus-
     tify keeping highly detailed and cross-referenced records.
 3. Table 8.1 is used in the explanation of all four methods in order to
     allow comparison of the effect that the different methods have on the
     dollar value of the ending inventory.

C. Solutions

Learning Unit 8.1

Determining the Inventory Balance

 1. 2 @ $22 = $ 44   2. 10 @ $23 = $230   3. 8 @ $25 = $200
     2 @ $24 = $ 48   2 @ $24 = $ 48   4 @ $22 = $ 88
     8 @ $23 = $184 $278 $288
               $276

4. 8 @ $25 = $ 200
   15 @ $22 = $ 330
   20 @ $20 = $ 400
   10 @ $24 = $ 240
   10 @ $23 = $ 230
   ——   ————
   63            $1,400

   $1,400/63 = $22.22
   $22.22 x 12 = $266.64

5. 4 @ $125 = $500
    1 @ $130 = $130
    1 @ $115 = $115
                 ————
                 $745

6. 6 @ $115 = $690

7. 2 @ $105 = $210
    4 @ $125 = $500
                ————
                $710

8.   2 x $105 = $ 210
    30 x $125 = $ 3,750
    20 x $128 = $ 2,560
    20 x $130 = $ 2,600
    10 x $115 = $ 1,150
    ——   ————————
    82            $10,270

    $10,270/82 = $125.24
    $125.24 x 6 = $751.44

9. 1 @ $ 84 = $ 84
    3 @ $ 85 = $ 255
    3 @ $ 90 = $ 270
    4 @ $100 = $ 400
    8 @ $ 95 = $ 760
                 ————————
                 $1,769

10. 10 @ $ 95 = $ 950
      8 @ $100 = $ 800
      1 @ $ 90 = $ 90
                   ————————
                   $1,840

11. 11 @ $80 = $ 880
      8 @ $84 = $ 672
                  ————————
                  $1,552

12. 11 @ $ 80 = $ 880
     10 @ $ 84 = $ 840
      5 @ $ 85 = $ 425
     15 @ $ 90 = $1,350
      8 @ $100 = $ 800
     10 @ $ 95 = $ 950
     ——   ————————
     59            $5,245

     $5,245/59 = $88.90
     $88.90 x 19 =
              $1,689.10

13. $70.00 < $72.00
    $70.00 x 5 = $350.00

14. $251.70

15. $330.00

16. $600.00

17. $364.00

18. $216.00

19. $239.60

20. $144.50

21. $45.00

22. $125.00

23.   11 @ $3.83 = $ 42.13
        10 @ $4.27 = $ 42.70
         5 @ $4.45 = $ 22.25
        10 @ $4.65 = $ 46.50
    (a) ——   (b) ————————
        36            $153.58

    (c) $153.58/36 = $4.27
        $4.27 x 13 = $55.51

24. 17 @ $181 = $ 3,077
     20 @ $194 = $ 3,880
     25 @ $203 = $ 5,075
     ——   ————————
     62           $12,032

     $12,032/62 = $194.06
     $194.06 x 29 = $5,627.74 average cost

```
          25 x $203 = $5,075.00
           4 x $194 = $  776.00
                      $5,851.00 FIFO

          17 x $181 = $3,077.00
          12 x $194 = $2,328.00
                      $5,405.00 LIFO
```

25. $ 577.60 = A
     $ 341.88 = D
     $ 239.46 = E
     $ 291.50 = G
     $ 244.80 = H
     $ 856.80 = J
     $ 2,552.04

Learning Unit 8.2

Determining the Cost

of Merchandise Sold

1. $313,244 + $4,000 = $317,244
    $317,244 - ($6,000 + $10,000) = $301,244

2. $109,800   3. $492,178   4. $54,836
5. $167,265   6. $93,875

7. $7,000 + $80,000 = $87,000
    $87,000 - $9,000 = $78,000

8. $127,210   9. $218,026   10. $180,655
11. $609,373   12. $71,343

13. $34,000 + net purchases = $396,544
    $396,544 - $34,000 = $362,544 (net purchases)

    $396,544 = $36,000 + cost of merchandise sold
    $396,544 - $36,000 = $360,544 (cost of merchandise sold)

14. $37,879; $22,334   15. $990,505; $93,761   16. $85,547; $80,146
17. $41,481; $355,701   18. $393,021; $25,198

19. $345,722 + $8,342 = $6,645 + $13,452 + net purchases
    $345,722 + $8,342 - $6,645 - $13,452 = $333,967 (net purchases)

20. $13,248   21. $1,102   22. $134,706
23. $25,244   24. $3,400

25. $ 45,678.13 $38,209.86 $505,846,31
     $455,778.22 $12,345.89 $ 59,424.40
     $ 4,389.96 $ 8,868.65 $446,421.91 cost of merchandise sold
     $505,846.31 $59,424.40

26. $ 3,977.34 $4,802.66 $57,732.86
        52,623.10   256.47   6,106.46
         1,132.42   1,047.33 $51,626.40 cost of merchandise sold
     $57,732.86 $6,106.46

Chapter 8
Self-Evaluation

1. (a) 1 @ $15 = $15
        2 @ 18 = 36
        2 @ 21 = 42
        ─   ────
        5                $93   Specific identification

   (b) FIFO: 5 x $21 = $105

   (c) LIFO: 4 @ $15 = $60
              1 @ 17 = 17
              ─   ────
              5          $77

   (d)   4 x $15 = $ 60 $756/40 = $18.90 each
         6 x 17 = 102   Average cost = 5 x $18.90 = $94.50
        12 x 18 = 216
        18 x 21 = 378
        ──   ────
        40          $756

2. (a) 24 x $4.60 = $110.40
   (b) 24 x $4.75 = $114.00
   (c) Lower = $110.40

3. $46,234.00
   - 1,058.35   ($824.35 + $234.00)
   ──────────
   $45,175.65

4. $ 33,542
   +145,675
   ────────
   $179,217
   - 46,732
   ────────
   $132,485   cost of merchandise sold

Chapter 9

Financial Statement Analysis

A. Purpose

This chapter explains how to use the income statement, balance sheet, and
bank reconciliation to analyze and interpret information about a business's
past performance and present financial condition. The computation and use
of financial ratios are also presented.

B. Comments

1. All percentages and ratios are rounded to the nearest hundredth.
2. Only major headings are presented in the income statement and balance
    sheet. The format presented for bank reconciliation is acceptable for
    business presentation. There is no generally accepted form for this
    cash control form.

C. Solutions

Learning Unit 9.1

Financial Statement Analysis

1. $124,000/$230,000 = .5391 = 53.91% $950/$230,000   = .0041 = 0.41%
   $35,200/$230,000 = .1530 = 15.30% $870/$230,000   = .0038 = 0.38%
   $37,800/$230,000 = .1643 = 16.43% $213,220/$230,000 = .9270 = 92.70%
   $4,700/$230,000 = .0204 = 2.04% $16,780/$230,000 = .0730 = 7.30%
   $5,100/$230,000 = .0222 = 2.22%
   $4,600/$230,000 = .0200 = 2.00%

2. $8,000/$173,200   = 4.62% $29,000/$173,200   = 16.74%
    $21,000/$173,200 = 12.12% $101,100/$173,200 = 58.37%
    $1,100/$173,200   = .64% $26,000/$173,200   = 15.01%
    $42,000/$173,200 = 24.25% $17,000/$173,200   = 9.82%
    $72,100/$173,200 = 41.63% $43,000/$173,200   = 24.83%
    $20,900/$173,200 = 12.07% $24,100/$173,200   = 13.91%
    $29,100/$173,200 = 16.80% $67,100/$173,200   = 38.74%
    $27,000/$173,200 = 15.59% $106,100/$173,200 = 61.26%
    $43,000/$173,200 = 24.83%

3. $192,300 - $188,000 = $43,000/$188,000 = .0229 = 2.29%
    ($3,000); (3.41%)
    $3,000; 7.69%
    $2,300; 16.20%
    $50; 2.33%
    $1,100; 21.57%
    ($100); (16.67%)
    $100; (14.29%)
    ($350); (28.00%)
    $2,900; 1.92%
    $1,400; 3.78%

4. $15,000 - $13,500 = $1,500/$13,500 = .1111 = 11.11%
    $800; 4.65%
    ($150); (17.65%)
    $1,400; 3.33%
    $3,550; 4.82%
    $1,400; 9.59%
    ($1,400); (4.46%)
    $2,000; 11.11%
    ($2,000); (6.25%)
    ($3,400); (3.85%)
    $150; 0.09%
    $5,500; 31.43%
    ($1,200); (6.25%)
    $4,300; 11.72%
    ($700); (1.74%)
    $3,600; 4.68%
    ($3,450); (7.64%)
    $150; 0.09%

Learning Unit 9.2

Financial Ratios

1. $84,000/$33,000 = 2.55:1
2. ($84,000 - $20,000)/$33,000 = 1.94:1
3. $120,000/$70,000 = 1.71:1
4. ($204,000 + $188,000)/2 = $196,000
    $20,000/$196,000 = .1020 = 10.2%
5. $20,000/$101,000 = .1980 = 19.8%
6. ($20,000 + $24,000)/2 = $22,000
    $80,000/$22,000 = 3.64
7. (a) $75,000/$72,000 = 1.04:1 (19-1)
        $84,000/$96,000 = 0.875:1 (19-2)
    (b) Acid test ratio
8. $140,000/$89,000 = 1.57:1 (19-1)
    $136,000/$82,000 = 1.66:1 (19-2)

9. ($275,000 + $235,000)/2 = $255,000
    $510,000/$255,000 = 2
10. (a) $240,000/$125,000 = 1.92:1 (Lube-All)
       $487,000/$236,000 = 2.06:1 (Global Oil)
    (b) Current ratio
11. $72,000/$600,000 = .12 = 12%
12. $35,000/$218,750 = .16 = 16%

Learning Unit 9.3

Bank Reconciliation

1. | | | |
    |---|---|---|
    | Balance per bank statement | | $ 1,025.40 |
    | Add: deposit in transit | | 730.00 |
    | | | $ 1,755.40 |
    | Deduct: outstanding checks | | 806.50 |
    | Adjusted balance | | $ 948.90 |
    | | | |
    | Balance per company records | | $ 955.80 |
    | Deduct: service charge | $2.90 | |
    | deposit box fee | 4.00 | 6.90 |
    | Adjusted balance | | $ 948.90 |

2. | | | |
    |---|---|---|
    | Balance per bank statement | | $ 3,761.62 |
    | Add: June 29 deposit | | 460.00 |
    | | | $ 4,221.62 |
    | Deduct: outstanding checks | | 283.43 |
    | Adjusted balance | | $ 3,938.19 |
    | | | |
    | Balance per company records | | $ 3,942.14 |
    | Add: error correction | | .80 |
    | | | $ 3,942.94 |
    | Deduct: service charge | $1.75 | |
    | note collection fee | 3.00 | 4.75 |
    | Adjusted balance | | $ 3,938.19 |

3. | | | |
    |---|---|---|
    | Balance per bank statement | | $10,023.61 |
    | Deduct: outstanding checks | | 1,807.24 |
    | Adjusted balance | | $ 8,216.37 |
    | | | |
    | Balance per company records | | $ 5,845.77 |
    | Add: note | $2,016 | |
    | deposit | 360 | 2,376.00 |
    | | | $ 8,221.77 |
    | Deduct: service charge | $3.40 | |
    | collection fee | 2.00 | 6.40 |
    | Adjusted balance | | $ 8,216.37 |

4. | | | |
    |---|---|---|
    | Balance per bank statement | | $ 9,319.35 |
    | Add: deposits | $1,190.00 | |
    | | 1,193.49 | 2,383.49 |
    | | | $11,702.84 |
    | Deduct: outstanding checks | | 3,919.07 |
    | Adjusted balance | | $ 7,783.77 |

```
        Balance per company records          $ 5,697.77
        Add:  note                             2,700.00
                                              $ 8,397.77

        Deduct:  service charge    $  9.00
                 collection fee       5.00
                 draft             600.00        614.00
        Adjusted balance                      $ 7,783.77
```

Chapter 9
Self-Evaluation

1. $77,000 - 43,000 = $34,000
   $34,000/43,000 = 79.07%

   $214,000 - 193,000 = $21,000
   $21,000/193,000 = 10.88%

   $291,000 - 236,000 = $55,000
   $55,000/236,000 = 23.31%

   $14,000 - 26,000 = ($12,000)
   ($12,000)/26,000 = (46.15%)

   $125,000 - 117,000 = $8,000
   $8,000/143,000 = 6.84%

   $139,000 - 143,000 = ($4,000)
   ($4,000)/143,000 = (2.80%)

   $152,000 - 93,000 = $59,000
   $59,000/93,000 = 63.44%

   $219,000 - 236,000 = $55,000
   $55,000/236,000 = 23.31%

2. $508,000/$781,000 = 65.04%

   $273,000/$781,000 = 34.96%

   $70,900/$781,000 = 9.08%

   $202,100/$781,000 = 25.88%

3. (a) $77,000/$14,000 = 5.5:1
   (b) ($77,000 - $15,000)/$14,000 = 4.43:1
   (c) $214,000/$125,000 = 1.71:1
   (d) ($291,000 + $236,000)/2 = $263,500
       $202,100/$263,500 = 76.70%
   (e) ($17,000 + $15,000)/2 = $16,000
       $102,000/$16,000 = 6.38 times

4.
```
   Bank balance                           $ 3,742.60
   Subtract:  outstanding checks              203.17
   Corrected balance                      $ 3,539.43

   Checkbook balance                      $ 3,096.01
   Add:  deposit                              450.00
         error correction                        .20
                                          $ 3,546.21
   Subtract:  service charge     $2.78
              note collection     4.00        6.78
   Corrected balance                      $ 3,539.43
```

Chapter 10

Distribution of Net Income

A.   Purpose

This chapter explains the three basic forms of business organization--sole
proprietorship, partnership, and corporation--as well as the advantages and
disadvantages of each form. The methods for distributing profit, according
to the way the business is organized, are presented.

B.   Comments

1. It should be emphasized that, in the absence of a written agreement in
    a partnership, the profits are distributed among the partners on an
    equal basis.
2. In discussing preferred stock, emphasize both the cumulative and parti-
    cipating aspects.

C.   Solutions

Learning Unit 10.1

Distribution of Net Income

for a Partnership

1. $47,000/3 = $15,700

2. $21,600

3. Spears, $24,600
    Tison, $36,900
    Young, $24,600

4. $98,120/11 = $8,920
    Cook, $8,920 x 5 = $44,600
    Collins, $8,920 x 3 = $26,760
    Case, $8,920 x 3 = $26,760

5. $28,000 + $14,000 + $42,000 = $84,000
   Jones, $67,140 x $28,000/$84,000 = $22,830
   Miles, $67,140 x $14,000/$84,000 = $11,190
   Moody, $67,140 x $42,000/$84,000 = $33,570

6. Kane, $34,605; Lott, $23,070; Lowe, $19,225.

7. $10,000 + $30,000 + $40,000 = $80,000 total investment
   ($9,000 + $9,000 + $9,000) - $11,160 = $15,840 excess withdrawn
   Pool, $15,840 x ($10,000/$80,000) = $1,980 share of excess
           $9,000 - $1,980 = $7,020 share of profit

   Wagner, $15,840 x ($30,000/$80,000) = $5,940 share of excess
           $9,000 - $5,940 = $3,060 share of profit

   Weems, $15,840 x ($40,000/$80,000) = $7,920 share of excess
           $9,000 - $7,920 = $1,080 share of profit

8. $36,000 + $24,000 + $20,000 = $80,000 total investment
   $63,500 - ($20,000 + $22,000) = $21,500 excess profit
   Phipps, $21,500 x ($36,000/$80,000) + $20,000 = $29,675
   McMeens, $21,500 x ($24,000/$80,000) + $22,000 = $28,450
   Harris, $21,500 x ($20,000/$80,000) = $5,375

9. Guy, $20,000 x .08 = $ 1,600   interest
                          10,000   salary
                           8,800   equal share
                         $20,400   total

   Nail, $28,000 x .08 = $ 2,240   interest
                          10,000   salary
                           8,800   equal share
                         $21,040   total

   Ross, $32,000 x .08 = $ 2,560   interest
                          10,000   salary
                           8,800   equal share
                         $21,360   total

10. Reel, $12,080; Roy, $10,680; Rood, $8,880.

11. (a) $23,000/2 = $11,500
    (b) $23,000/5 = $4,600
        Townly, $4,600 x 2 = $9,200
        Thomas, $4,600 x 3 = $13,800
    (c) Townly, $23,000 x ($40,000/$100,000) = $9,200
        Thomas, $23,000 x ($60,000/$100,000) = $13,800

    (d) Townly, $15,000   salary
                  -(2,000) excess withdrawal
                  $13,000   total

        Thomas, $12,000   salary
                  -(2,000) excess withdrawal
                  $10,000   total

Learning Unit 10.2

Distribution of Net Income

for a Corporation

1. $64,000/30,000 = $2.13
2. Preferred, $5.00; common ($50,000 - $10,000)/$10,000 = $4.00.
3. Common, ($150,000 - $50,000)/100,000 = $1.00
    Preferred, $100 x .05 = $5.00 ($50,000 total)
4. Common, $3.25; preferred, $4.00 ($100,000 total).
5. Common, $5.00 + $2.00 participating = $7.00
    Preferred, $5.00 + $2.00 participating = $7.00
6. Common, $3.11; preferred, $5.00 ($125,000 total).
7. Common, $3.00; preferred, $8.00 ($120,000 total).
8. Common, $3.35; preferred, $7.50.
9. Common, $307,000 - $100,000 = $207,000
    Preferred, $80 x .05 = $4.00 + $1.00 = $5.00
                20,000 x $5.00 = $100,000 total
10. Common, $102,000; preferred, $36,000.
11. Common, $109,000; preferred, $43,600.
12. Common, $450,000; preferred, $500,000.
13. Common, $73,250; preferred, $0.
14. Common, $250,000 x 4 = $1,000,000 + $187,500 = $1,187,500

    Preferred, $100 x .08 = $8.00
                50,000 x $8.00 = $400,000
                50,000 x .75 =   37,500
                               $437,500 total

15. Common, $1,512,000; preferred, $1,260,000.
16. Common, $18,800; preferred, $56,000.
17. $45,000 - $24,000 = $21,000 for dividends
    (a) $21,000/18,500 = $1.14
    (b) Preferred, $80 x .06 = $4.80 per share
                $4.80 x 3,000 = $14,400
        Common, ($21,000 - $14,400)/15,000 = $0.44 per share
18. Preferred, $100 x .07 = $7.00
                4,000 x $7 = $28,000 total
    (a) First year, $14,000/4,000 = $3.50 per share
    (b) Second year, $7 + $3.50 = $10.50
                $10.50 x 4,000 = $42,000
        Common, ($50,000 - $42,000)/50,000 = $0.16
    (c) Preferred, $100 x .07 = $7.00
                4,000 x $7 = $28,000 total
        Common, ($228,000 - $28,000)/50,000 = $4.00 per share
19. $1,360,000 x .40 = $544,000 dividends
    (a) Common, $544,000
    (b) Preferred, $100 x .05 = $5.00 + $0.70 = $5.70
                50,000 x $5.70 = $285,000
        Common, $1.89 + $0.70 = $2.59
                100,000 x $2.59 = $259,000

                50,000 x $5 = $250,000
                100,000 x $1.89   189,000
                                 $439,000

        ($544,000 - $439,000)/150,000 = $0.70 per share
    (c) Cumulative preferred, $3.00 + $3.00 = $6.00
                10,000 x $6 = $60,000

```
        Preferred, $80 x .05 = $4.00
                  40,000 x $4 = $160,000
        Common, $544,000 - ($160,000 + $60,000) = $324,000
```

Chapter 10
Self-Evaluation

1. $39,780/2 = $19,890 each

2.

Justin	Mallory	Timmons
	$ 8,000	$14,000
$17,000	10,200	6,800
$17,000	$18,200	$20,800

   $56,000 - $22,000 = $34,000/10 = $3,400
   $3,400 x 5; $3,400 x 3; $3,400 x 2

3. $50,000   Travis, 50,000/80,000 x $48,864 = $30,540
    30,000
   $80,000   Duke, 30,000/80,000 x $48,864 = $18,324

4. Elam, $30,000 x .10 = $3,000 + $13,670.00 = $16,670.00
   Goodner, $50,000 x .10 = $5,000 + $13,670.00 = $18,670.00
   Drake, $20,000 x .10 = $2,000 + $13,670.00 = $15,670.00
   51,010 - $10,000 = $41,010/3 = $13,670.00

5. Preferred, $100 x .06 = $6 x 6,000 = $36,000
   Common, $236,000 - $36,000 = $200,000

6. $85,000 x .60 = $51,000
   $100 x .06 - $6 x 3,000 = $18,000
   $51,000 - $18,000 = $33,000

7.

```
   $1,238,000      $1,200,000
   -    38,000     -   360,000
   $1,200,000      $   840,000
          .30
   $   360,000
```

   $80 x .05 = 4 cum pf
   $4 + $1 = $5 x 4,000 = $20,000

   $7.00 pf
   10,000 x $7 = $70,000

   ($84,000 - $20,000 - $70,000)/1,000,000 = $.75 common

Chapter 11

Short-Term Credit

A.   Purpose

Businesses usually acquire goods and services on credit rather than through
immediate cash payments. In the short term, promissory notes are used in
borrowing and lending money. This chapter presents the techniques for calculating simple interest and bank discount.

B.   Comments

 1. When solving the simple interest formula for principal, the answer is
     present value at simple interest and can be used as a good approxima-
     tion for present value at compound interest.
 2. The differences between simple interest and bank discount should be
     emphasized.
 3. Since this text is not specifically designed to be used with a calcula-
     tor, a 360-day year is used in many of the examples to make calculation
     by hand easier and faster.

C.   Solutions

Learning Unit 11.1

Simple Interest

 1. $3,000 x .06 x 36/360 = $18.00
 2. $87.50   3. $128.89   4. $21.00   5. $733.33
 6. $50.38   7. $108.50   8. $91.35   9. $48.33
10. $27.87   11. $25.88   12. $132.00

13. $15.85   14. $3.85   15. $38.00
16. $800 x .08 x 90/365 = $15.78
17. $44.38   18. $27.33   19. $733.56
20. $684.62   21. $195.96   22. $24.00
23. $65.75   24. $4.32   25. $37.07
26. $600 x .07 x 60/360 = $7.00 ordinary
    $600 x .07 x 60/365 = $6.90 exact
                          $ .10 difference

27. $26.00; $25.64; $.36   28. $352.00; $347.18; $4.82
29. $240.83; $237.53; $3.30   30. $8.11; $8.00; $.11

31. $12,542 x .08 x 90/365 = $247.40
    $12,542 + $247.40 = $12,789.40
32. $500 x .06 x 120/365 = $9.86
    $500 + $9.86 = $509.86
33. $300 x .07 x 4/12 = $7.00
34. $5,000 x .11 x 90/365 = $135.62
35. $9,000 x .12 x 120/365 = $355.07
36. $22,500 x .09 x 6/12 = $1,012.50
    $22,500 + $1,012.50 = $23,512.50
37. $3,500 x .09 x 18/12 = $472.50
    $3,500 + $472.50 = $3,972.50
38. $6,000 x .11 x 4 = $2,640
    $6,000 + $2,640 = $8,640

Learning Unit 11.2

Finding the Principal,

Rate, and Time

1. $P = \dfrac{I}{R \times T} = \dfrac{\$80}{.08 \times 90/360} = \dfrac{\$80}{.02} = \$4,000.00$

2. $800.00   3. $960.00   4. $1,230.00
5. $8,340.00   6. $9,270.00

7. $R = \dfrac{I}{P \times T} = \dfrac{\$100}{\$5,000 \times 60/360} = \dfrac{\$100}{\$833.33} = .12 = 12\%$

8. 12%   9. 3%   10. 6.5%   11. 9.3%   12. 5%

13. $T = \dfrac{I}{P \times R} = \dfrac{\$14}{\$2,000 \times .07} = \dfrac{\$14}{\$140} = .1$ years = 36 days

14. 60 days   15. 45 days   16. 320 days
17. 15 days   18. 120 days

19. $\dfrac{\$75}{\$2,500 \times .06} = .5$ years = 180 days

20. $\dfrac{\$100}{\$2,500 \times 6/12} = .08 = 8\%$

21. $\dfrac{\$1,200}{.06 \times 1} = \$20,000$

22. $\dfrac{\$150}{\$7,500 \times 90/360} = .08 = 8\%$

23. $\dfrac{\$600}{.05 \times 120/360} = \$36,000$

24. $\dfrac{\$500}{\$13,000 \times 120/360} = .115 = 11.5\%$

25. $\dfrac{\$187.50}{\$15,000 \times .05} = .25$ years $= 90$ days

26. $\dfrac{\$27}{.09 \times 90/360} = \$1,200$

Learning Unit 11.3

Bank Discount

1. Table method: (1) May 10 = Day # 130

$$\begin{array}{r} 130 \\ +90 \\ \hline 220 \end{array}$$

   (2) Day # 220 = August 8
2. March 24, 1979   3. July 7, 1980   4. October 5, 1979
5. March 6, 1981   6. May 20, 1979   7. May 18, 1981
8. September 26, 1980   9. February 12, 1980   10. May 22, 1981
11. $3,000 \times .09 \times 80/365 = \$59.18$
    $3,000 - \$59.18 = \$2,940.82$
12. $30.25; \$889.75   13. \$17.20; \$1,362.80   14. \$79.69; \$1,820.31
15. $94.03; \$1,205.97   16. \$240.49; \$3,559.51
17. $798.90; \$11,201.10   18. \$497.26; \$10,502.74
19. $13.17; \$749.83   20. \$3.94; \$475.05

21. (1) March 6 = Day # 65

$$\begin{array}{r} 65 \\ +60 \\ \hline 125 \end{array}$$

   (2) Day # 125 = May 5
   (3) $2,000 \times .08 \times 60/365 = \$26.30$
       $2,000 + \$26.30 = \$2,026.30$

22. July 13, 1979; $4,098.63   23. March 7, 1980; \$966.12
24. July 25, 1980; $6,118.64   25. December 14, 1981; \$2,217.39
26. April 14, 1981; $7,849.64   27. June 30, 1980; \$4,351.03
28. August 8, 1980; $3,168.79   29. June 27, 1981; \$1,260.21
30. September 15, 1980; $2,149.02
31. (1) $5,000 \times .07 \times 60/365 = \$57.53$ (interest)
    (2) $5,000 + \$57.53 = \$5,057.53$ (maturity value)
    (3) August 1 = Day # 213
        July 22 = Day # −203
                      10 days held prior to discount

    (4) 60 − 10 = 50 days (discount period)
    (5) $5,057.53 \times .085 \times 50/365 = \$58.89$ discount
    (6) $5,057.53 − \$58.89 = \$4,998.64$ net proceeds
32. $38.62; \$1,603.46   33. \$45.59; \$3,217.53
34. $137.17; \$4,771.43   35. \$46.86; \$8,002.46
36. $7.39; \$899.82   37. \$53.16; \$2,800.35
38. $25.32; \$2,149.42   39. \$84.46; \$12,004.31
40. $154.65; \$4,272.58

Chapter 11
Self-Evaluation

1. I = \$2,200/1 x 9/100 x 60/360 = \$33.00
2. I = \$3,000/1 x 10/100 x 73/365 = \$60.00

3. (a) $R = \dfrac{\$12}{\dfrac{\$800}{1} \times \dfrac{90}{360}} = \dfrac{\$12}{\dfrac{800}{6}}$ = 12/1 x 6/800 = 72/800 = 9/100 = 9%

    (b) $P = \dfrac{\$50}{\dfrac{8}{100} \times \dfrac{90}{360}} = \dfrac{\$50}{\dfrac{1}{50}}$ = \$50/1 x 50/1 = \$2,500

    (c) I = \$1,440/1 x 9/100 x 60/360 = \$32.40

    (d) $R = \dfrac{\$13}{\dfrac{\$1,300}{1} \times \dfrac{30}{360}} = \dfrac{\$13}{\dfrac{\$1,300}{12}}$ = 13/1 x 12/1,300 = 12/100 = 12%

4. (a) May 17 = day # 137   (b) Nov. 1 = day #   305
                  +60 days   +100 days
        day # 197 = July 16   405
                                      (Dec. 31) # -365
                                        day #   40 = Feb. 9

5. BD = \$3,700/1 x 8/100 x 80/365 = \$4,736/73 = \$64.88
    NP = \$3,700 - \$64.88 = \$3,635.12

6. (a) June 7 = day # 158
                  +90 days
        day # 248 = September 5

    (b) I = \$7,000/1 x 8/100 x 90/365 = \$10,080/73 = \$138.08
        MV = \$7,000 + \$138.08 = \$7,138.08
7. I = \$2,700/1 x 8/100 x 150/365 = \$32,400/365 = \$88.77;
    MV = \$2,788.77
    BD = \$2,788.77/1 x 10/100 x *120/365 = \$91.69

    *July 22 - Aug. 21 = 30 days
    150 - 30 = 120 days left

    NP = \$2,788.77 - \$91.69 = \$2,697.08

Chapter 12

The Time Value

of Money

A. Purpose

Money that is borrowed pays a simple rate of interest; however, money that
is invested normally earns compound interest--the interest also earns interest. This chapter is designed to help the student understand and use compound interest, present value, ordinary annuities, sinking funds, and
amortization.

B. Comments

1. The use of tables for compound interest, present value, and ordinary
    annuities allows the student to continue to build arithmetic skills by
    not requiring a calculator.
2. Methods of calculating the other types of annuities mentioned in this
    chapter are basically similar to those used to calculate the ordinary
    annuity.

C. Solutions

Learning Unit 12.1

Compound Interest

1. $1,800 x .08 x 6/12 = $72.00
    $1,872 x .08 x 6/12 = $74.88
    $72.00 + $74.88 = $146.88
2. $252.99   3. $744.41   4. $1,813.57   5. $2,258.89
6. $1,000 x 1.06136355 = $1,061.36
    $1,061.36 - $1,000 = $61.36
7. $1,325.38; $125.38   8. $6,400.42; $1,400.42

9. $8,308.59; $2,108.59   10. $21,050.82; $7,050.82
11. $27,891.51; $10,591.51   12. $3,056.03; $1,156.03
13. $5,161.01; $1,861.01   14. $5,839.19; $1,139.19
15. $135,849.63; $73,849.63
16. (a) 1.51644279 x $3,000 = $4,549.33
    (b) 1.74221349 x $3,000 = $5,226.64
    (c) 1.93333841 x $3,000 = $5,800.02
17. 1.26973465 x $25,000 = $31,743.37
    $31,743.37 - $25,000 = $6,743.37
18. 1.41297382 x $5,000 = $7,064.87
19. (a) 1.21988955 x $6,000 = $7,319.34
    (b) $7,319.34 - $6,000 = $1,319.34

Learning Unit 12.2

Finding the Principal,

Rate, and Time

1. $MV/P = (1 + i)^n$

    $\$3,000/\$1,000 = (1 + i)^{28}$

    $3 = (1 + i)^{28}$
    $i = 4.5\%*$
    $I = 4 \times 4.5\% = 18\%$
2. 14%   3. 9%   4. 8%   5. 6%   6. 8%
7. $MV/P = (1 + i)^n$

    $2,800/1,200 = (1 + .03)^n$

    $2.33333333 = (1 + .03)^n$

    $n = 29 = 7\ 1/4$ yr.
8. 4 1/2 yrs.   9. 3 yrs.   10. 5 1/4 yrs.
11. 3 1/3 yrs.   12. 10 years
13. $MV/P = (1 + i)^n$

    $\$4,250/\$2,000 = (1 + .025)^n$

    $2.125 = (1.025)^n$
    $n = 31 = 4\ 3/4$ yr. or 4 years, nine months
14. 12 years   15. 7%   6. 15%

Learning Unit 12.3

Present Value

1. $2,000 x .92455621 = $1,849.11
2. $3,358.48   3. $3,248.23   4. $4,103.73   5. $4,728.95
6. $3,934.78   7. $1,228.63   8. $4,183.87   9. $10,338.74
10. $31,159.08   11. $20,046.15   12. $44,706.21
13. $16,861.54   14. $13,483.67
15. (a) .72844581 x $4,300 = $3,132.32
    (b) .88848705 x $2,380 = $2,114.60
    (c) .70682458 x $10,127 = $7,158.01

* Using tables provided in this book, 4.5% is the lowest i value that will
give the desired MV in seven years. Other tables with a greater number of
possible i values would designate a lower i value.

16. .50256588 x $100,000 = $50,256.59
17. .45638695 x $50,000 = $22,819.35
18. $\underline{i}$ = 6/4 = 1 1/2%
     $\underline{n}$ = 4 x 12 = 48
     $\overline{PV}$ = $16,000 x (.48936170)
     $\overline{PV}$ = $7,829.79
19. $\underline{i}$ = 10/4 = 2 1/2%
     $\underline{n}$ = 4 x 10 = 40
     $\overline{PV}$ = $50,000 x (.37243062)
     $\overline{PV}$ = $18,621.53

Learning Unit 12.4

Annuities

 1. $\underline{MV}$ = $\underline{P}$ x $\overline{Sn}|i$
     $\underline{i}$ = 1%
     $\underline{n}$ = 42
     $\overline{MV}$ = $100(51.87898946)
     $\overline{MV}$ = $5,187.90

 2. $15,210.93   3. $11,977.99   4. $5,961.25   5. $20,220.77

 6. $\underline{PV}$ = $\underline{P}$ x $\overline{An}|i$
     $\underline{i}$ = 6%
     $\underline{n}$ = 8
     $\overline{PV}$ = $2,500(6.20979381)
     $\overline{PV}$ = $15,524.48

 7. $4,018.48   8. $5,016.31   9. $5,029.62   10. $6,247.64
11. $\underline{MV}$ = $\underline{P}$ x $\overline{Sn}|i$, $\underline{i}$ = 2%, $\underline{n}$ = 18
     $\overline{MV}$ = $300 (21.41231238); $\underline{MV}$ = $6,423.69
12. $\underline{MV}$ = $\underline{P}$ x $\overline{Sn}|i$, $\underline{i}$ = .5%, $\underline{n}$ = 48
     $\overline{MV}$ = $100 (54.09783222); $\underline{MV}$ = $5,409.78
13. $\underline{MV}$ = $\underline{P}$ x $\overline{Sn}|i$, $\underline{i}$ = 7%, $\underline{n}$ = 13
     $\overline{MV}$ = $2,000 (20.14064286); $\underline{MV}$ = $40,281.29
14. $\underline{MV}$ = $\underline{P}$ x $\overline{Sn}|i$, $\underline{i}$ = 8%, $\underline{n}$ = $\overline{7}$
     $\overline{MV}$ = $1,800 (8.92280336); $\underline{MV}$ = $16,061.05
15. $\underline{PV/P}$ = $\overline{An}|i$; $\underline{i}$ = 2%, $5,000/$300 = $\overline{An}|$ .02; 16.66666667 = $\overline{An}|$.02
     $\underline{n}$ = 20
16. $\underline{PV/P}$ = $\overline{An}|i$; $\underline{i}$ = 1 1/4%, $12,000/$400 = $\overline{An}|$ .0125; 30 = $\overline{An}|$ .0125
     $\underline{n}$ = 37
17. $\underline{PV}$ = $\underline{P}$ x $\overline{An}|i$, $\underline{i}$ = 2%, $\underline{n}$ = 44
     $\overline{PV}$ = $950 (29.07996307)
     $\overline{PV}$ = $27,625.96
     Equivalent cash price = $27,625.96 + $10,000 down = $37,625.96
18. $\underline{PV}$ = $\underline{P}$ x $\overline{An}|i$, $\underline{i}$ = .5%, $\underline{n}$ = 48
     $\overline{PV}$ = $250 (42.58031778)
     $\overline{PV}$ = $10,645.08
19. $\underline{MV}$ = $\underline{P}$ x $\overline{Sn}|i$, $\underline{i}$ = 2%, $\underline{n}$ = 48
     $\overline{MV}$ = $500 (79.35351927)
     $\overline{MV}$ = $39,676.76
20. $\underline{MV}$ = $\underline{P}$ x $\overline{Sn}|i$, $\underline{i}$ = 4%, $\underline{n}$ = 10
     $\overline{MV}$ = $1,000 (12.00610712)
     $\overline{MV}$ = $12,006.11

Learning Unit 12.5

Sinking Funds

and Amortization

1. $i = 2\%$; $n = 28$; $P = \$80,000 \times .02698967$; $P = \$2,159.17$
2. $i = 3\%$; $n = 24$; $P = \$30,000 \times .02904742$; $P = \$871.42$
3. $i = 5\%$; $n = 20$; $P = \$75,000 \times .03024259$; $P = \$2,268.19$
4. $i = 2.5\%$; $n = 24$; $P = \$14,000 \times .03091282$; $P = \$432.78$
5. $i = 4.5\%$; $n = 30$; $P = \$25,000 \times .01639154$; $P = \$409.79$
6. $i = 3\%$; $n = 12$; $P = \$110,000 \times .07046209$; $P = \$7,750.83$
7. $i = 3.5\%$; $n = 20$; $P = \$42,000 \times .03536108$; $P = \$1,485.17$
8. $i = 6\%$; $n = 8$; $P = \$8,000 \times .10103594$; $P = \$808.29$

	r	n	$P = MV \times 1/Sn\rceil i$	P	Total Payments	Interest
9.	2%	16	$P = \$21,000 \times .05365013$	$1,126.65	$18.026.40	$2,973.60
10.	1%	24	$P = \$6,000 \times .03707347$	$ 222.44	$ 5,338.56	$ 661.44
11.	2.5%	34	$P = \$18,000 \times .01900675$	$ 342.12	$11,632.08	$6,367.92
12.	.75%	48	$P = \$11,000 \times .01738504$	$ 191.24	$ 9;179.52	$1,820.48
13.	1.75%	20	$P = \$36,000 \times .04219122$	$1,518.83	$30,376.60	$5,623.40
14.	1.5%	32	$P = \$150,000 \times.02457710$	$3,686.57	$117,970.24	$32,029.76
15.	.75%	36	$P = \$28,000 \times .02429973$	$ 680.39	$24,494.04	$3,505.96
16.	1.5%	16	$P = \$17,500 \times .05576508$	$ 975.89	$15,614.24	$1,885.76

17. $i = 3\%$; $n = 40$; $P = \$30,000 \times .04326238 = \$1,297.87$
18. $i = 2\%$; $n = 12$; $P = \$8,000 \times .09455960 = \$756.48$
19. $i = 8\%$; $n = 15$; $P = \$60,000 \times .11682954 = \$7,009.77$
20. $i = 2.5\%$; $n = 16$; $P = \$100,000 \times .07659899 = \$7,659.90$
21. $i = 1.75\%$; $n = 40$; $P = \$24,000 \times .03497209 = \$839.33$
22. $i = 2\%$; $n = 16$; $P = \$5,200 \times .07365013 = \$382.98$
23. $i = 4.5\%$; $n = 26$; $P = \$32,000 \times .06602137 = \$2,112.68$
24. $i = 1\%$; $n = 48$; $P = \$50,000 \times .02633384 = \$1,316.69$

	r	n	$P = PV \times 1/An\rceil i$	P	Total Repaid	Interest
25.	2%	40	$P = \$40,000 \times .03655575$	$ 146.22	$ 5,848.80	$ 1,848.80
26.	5%	36	$P = \$15,000 \times .06043446$	$ 906.52	$ 32,634.72	$17,634.72
27.	.5%	30	$P = \$14,500 \times .03597892$	$ 521.69	$ 15,650.70	$ 1,150.70
28.	4.5%	40	$P = \$25,000 \times .05434315$	$ 1,358.58	$ 54,343.20	$29,343.20
29.	7%	6	$P = \$9,400 \times .20979580$	$ 1,972.08	$ 11,832.48	$ 2,432.48
30.	.75%	42	$P = \$87,000 \times .02784452$	$ 2,422.47	$101,743.74	$14,743.74
31	5%	5	$P = \$50,000 \times .23097480$	$11,548.74	$ 57,743.70	$ 7,743.70
32.	2.5%	40	$P = \$32,000 \times .03983623$	$ 1,274.76	$ 50,990.40	$18,990.40

33. $i = 4\%$; $n = 40$; $P = \$500,000 \times .01052349 = \$5,261.75$
34. $i = .75\%$; $n = 48$
   (a) $P = \$8,000 \times .01738504 = \$139.08$
   (b) $\$8,000 - \$6,675 = \$1,324.16$ interest
   (c) $48 \times \$139.08 = \$6,675.84$ deposits
35. $i = 2\%$; $n = 40$
   (a) $P = \$1,000,000 \times .01655575 = \$16,555.75$
   (b) $\$1,000,000 - \$662,230 = \$337,770$ interest
   (c) $40 \times \$16,555.75 = \$662,230.00$ deposits
36. $\$7,500 - \$1,500 = \$6,000$
   $i = 1\%$; $n = 48$
   $P = \$6,000 \times .02633384 = \$158.00$ per month

37. $r = .75\%$; $n = 36$
    (a) $P = \$5,000 \times .03179973 = \$159.00$ per month
    (b) $\$5,724 - \$50,000 = \$724$ interest

38. $r = 6\%$; $n = 40$
    (a) $P = \$40,000 \times .06646154 = \$2,658.46$ payment
    (b) $\$106,338.40 - \$40,000 = \$66,338.40$ interest
    (c) $40 \times \$2,658.46 = \$106,338.40$ total cost

Chapter 12
Self-Evaluation

1. $I = \$1,600 \times 6/100 \times 1/4 =$ $\$24.00$
    $I = \$1,624/1 \times 6/100 \times 1/4 =$ 24.36
    $I = \$1,648.36/1 \times 6/100 \times 1/4 =$ 24.73 (rounded)
    $I = \$1,673.09/1 \times 6/100 \times 1/4 =$ 25.10
                                 $\$98.19$ total interest

2. $MV = \$2,700 \times 1.17165938$; $MV = \$3,163.48$
3. $MV = \$3,100 \times 1.61222608$; $MV = \$4,997.90$

4. $2/1 = (1 + r)^{26}$; $r = 2\ 3/4\%$; $R = 4 \times 2\ 3/4\% = 11\%$

5. $\$4,500/1,500 = (1 + .05)^{n}$; $3 = (1 + .05)^{n}$; $n = 23$ or $11\ 1/2$ years
6. $PV = \$1,800 \times .76789574$; $PV = \$1,382.21$
7. $PV = \$12,000 \times .67362493$; $PV = \$8,083.50$
8. $PV = \$17,000 \times .78756613$; $PV = \$13,388.62$
9. $MV = P \cdot S\overline{n}|i$; $MV = \$200\ (57.52071111)$; $MV = \$11,504.14$
10. $PV = P \cdot A\overline{n}|i$; $PV = \$500 \times 10.57534122$; $PV = \$5,287.67$
11. $PV = P \cdot A\overline{n}|i$; $\$7,000/\$300 = A\overline{n}|1\%$; $23.33333333 = A\overline{n}|1\%$; $n = 26$
12. (a) $P = \$250,000 \times .01260184$; $P = \$3,150.46$ ($r = 2\%$; $n = 48$)
    (b) $48 \times \$3,150.46\ \$151,222.08$ deposits
    (c) $\$250,000 - \$151,222.08 = \$98,777.92$ interest
13. (a) $P = \$14,000 \times .02488504$; $P = \$348.39$ ($r = 3/4\%$; $n = 48$)
    (b) $\$16,722.72 - \$14,000 = \$2,722.72$
    (c) $\$348.39 \times 48 = \$16,722.72$

Chapter 13

Consumer Credit

A. Purpose

One of the basic services business offers to consumers is the buying of goods and services on credit. As in the case of most other services, business usually passes the cost of credit transactions on to the consumer. Federal, state, and local governments have all worked to establish some consistency for reporting costs to the consumer. This chapter presents the calculation and reporting of credit and discusses the operation of the more popular credit plans.

B. Comments

1. Complete tables and information for credit disclosure are available from government publications.
2. The open-end account is emerging as one of the more important credit plans.

C. Solutions

Learning Unit 13.1

Installment Loans

1. $38/$528 = .07198 x 100 = 7.198 and 12 months = 13%
2. 11.75%   3.   15.5%   4.   9.75%
5. 16 %   6.   17.5%   7.   10.75%
8. 8.5%   9.   17%   10.   12.25%
11. $42 x 12 + $50 = $554 - $500 = $54
     $54/($500 - $50) = .12 x 100 = 12.000 for 12 months = 21.5%

60

12. $60; 12.75%
13. $8 x 6 + ($55 x .20) = $59 - $55 = $4
    $4/($55 - $11) = 0.09091 x 100 = 9.091 for 8 months = 23.75%
14. $9; 17.5%   15. $24; 17.25%   16. $79.70; 20.5%   17. $20; 28%
18. $98; 20.5%   19. $3.05; 24.25%   20. $10; 20.25%
21. $92/$460 = .2 x 100 = 20 for 15 months = 28.5%
22. $42/$300 = .14 x 100 = 14.00 for 12 months = 25%
23. $40 x 24 + ($870 x .10) = $1,047 - $870 = $177
    $177/($870 - $87) = .22605 x 100 = 22.605 for 24 months = 20.5%
24. $50 x 10 + $50 = $550 - $500 = $50
    $50/($500 - $50) = .11111 = 11.11 for 10 months = 23.5%
25. $30/$450 = .06667 x 100 = 6.667 for 9 months = 15.75%
    $128/$800 = .16 x 100 = 16 for 20 months = 17.5%
    $65/$625 = .104 x 100 = 10.4 for 24 months = 9.75%
    $175/$1,500 = .11667 x 100 = 11.667 for 18 months = 14.25%
    $24/$300 = .08 x 100 = 8 for 12 months = 14.5%

Learning Unit 13.2

Open-End Charge Accounts

1. $214 x .01 = $2.14
   $214 + $2.14 - $50 = $166.14 balance
   1% x 12 = 12% APR
2. $151.90; 12%   3. $136; 18%   4. $250.33; 18%
5. $78.70; 21%   6. $101.25; 12%   7. $65.30; 21%
8. $27.55; 9%   9. $85.55; 18%   10. $11.69; 18%
11. $146 x .015 = $2.19
    $146 + $2.19 + $32 - $20 = $160.19
12. $106.18   13. $160.89   14. $89.18
15. $88.98   16. $216.41   17. $378.75
18. $445.35   19. $557.95   20. $486.32
21. $180.65 x .0133 = $2.40
    $180.65 + $2.40 - $40 = $143.05
22. $93 x .015 = $1.40
    $93 + $1.40 + $119.95 - $50 = $164.35

Chapter 13
Self-Evaluation

1. $28/$360 x 100 = 7.78 for 10 payments = 16.50%
2. $50/$600 x 100 = 8.33 for 12 payments = 15.00%
3. $50 + (10 x $15) = $200 - $180 = $20 finance charge
   $20/$130 x 100 = 15.38 for 10 payments = 32.25%
4. $25 + (12 x $20) = $265 - $235 = $30 finance charge
   $30/$210 x 100 = 14.29 for 12 payments = 25.50%
5. $187 + $2.49 - $40 = $149.49
   1 1/3% x 12 = 16%
6. $519.67 + $7.80 - $120.00 + $65.30 = $472.77

Chapter 14

Investments

A.   Purpose

Although investments in stocks or bonds carry a greater risk than some other
types of investment, there is a reasonable expectation for a satisfactory
return over a period of years.   This material investigates the terminology,
indices, and procedures for evaluating stock and bond investments.

B.   Comments

1.   Emphasis on terminology is essential to understanding stock and bond
     investment.
2.   The purchasing of stocks is equity financing for the issuing corpora-
     tion and does not have to be repaid.
3.   The purchasing of bonds is debt financing for the issuing corporation
     and must be repaid along with interest.

C.   Solutions

Learning Unit 14.1

Investment in Stocks

1. $30.625   2. $46.75   3. $32.125   4. $1.50
5. $104.125   6. $16.25   7. $17.875   8. $29.375
9. $14.875   10. $16.75   11. $45.75   12. $44.625
13. $126,000/90,000 = $1.40
14. $0.28   15. $1.96   16. $2.40
17. $0.64   18. $2.16   19. $0.44

62

20. $11.52   21. $0.96   22. $2.20
23. P-E ratio, $17.00/1.35 = 13
    Dividend yield, ($1.35 x .80)/$17 = .06 = 6%
24. 22; 4%   25. 17; 5%   26. 22; 4%
27. 18; 4%   28. 33; 2%   29. 11; 8%
30. 14; 6%   31. $45.875   32. $11.125
33. ($150,000 - $30,000)/140,000 = $0.86
34. $26/$1.60 = 16
35. $0.56/$24.00 = .02 = 2%

Learning Unit 14.2

Investment in Bonds

1. $1,000 x .98 = $980 current price
   $1,000 x .1075 = $107.50 annual interest
2. $772.50; $32.50   3. $870.00; $30.00   4. $895.00; $55.00
5. $837.50; $73.75   6. $788.75; $60.00   7. $935.00; $50.00
8. $852.50; $65.00   9. $795.00; $61.00   10. $537.50; $50.00
11. $730.00; $45.00   12. $875.00; $60.00
13. Discount   14. High
15. $1,000 x 1.01375 = $1,013.75
    $1,000 x .087 = $87.00
    $87.00/$1,013.75 = .086 = 8.6%
16. 8.8%   17. 9%   18. 8.2%
19. 61.5%   20. 9.1%

21. $1,000 x .96 = $960.00
    $1,000 x .08 x 1/4 =   20.00
                          $980.00 total cost

22. $561.88   23. $1,033.44   24. $1,008.33

25. $1,000 x .75 = $750.00 current price
    $1,000 x .04 = $40.00
    $40.00/$750.00 = .053 = 5.3% current yield
    $40.00/2 = $20 semiannual interest

26. $1,000 x .99375 = $993.75
27. $1,000 x .975 = $975.00
28. $1,000 x .05 = $50.00
    $50/$580.00 = .086 = 8.6%

Chapter 14
Self-Evaluation

1. 11 5/8 = $11.625
2. $58,750/47,000 = $1.25
3. $25.375/$1.40 = 18
4. $1.40/$25.375 = .055 = 5.5%
5. 1.145 x $1,000 = $1,145
6. $1,000 x .0625/2 = $31.25
7. .92875 x $1,000 = $928.75

Chapter 15

The Mathematics of Real Estate

A.   Purpose

This chapter explains some specific aspects of real estate activity: the
compensation paid brokers for handling real estate sales transactions; the
points involved in financing real estate; the taxes levied on real property
by various units of local government; and percentage leases involved in the
rental of shopping centers, stores, and offices used by businesses. After
completing this chapter, the student should be able to explain the meaning
of various terms used in the real estate industry, calculate the amount of
commission on real estate transactions, compute the rate of commission or
price of the property on real estate transactions, determine the cost of
title insurance, calculate loan origination costs on real estate transactions, demonstrate an understanding of how real estate taxes are levied,
calculate real estate taxes, and determine the total rent paid or percentage
rate on a percentage lease.

B.   Comments

  1.   Several terms presented in this chapter are not familiar to many stu-
        dents and should be explained and illustrated by the instructor.
  2.   This chapter provides another opportunity for the student to use the
        basic percentage formula ($\underline{P} = \underline{B} \times \underline{R}$) when calculating a real estate
        broker's commission.

64

C.   Solutions

Learning Unit 15.1

Real Estate Commissions

1. $106,000 x .06 = $6,360   2. $3,780
3. $3,350   4. $1,760   5. $2,990   6. $4,900
7. $74,000 x .05 = $3,700   8. $3,710; $1,484
    $3,700 x .5 = $1,850
9. $2,160; $1,296   10. $3,355; $1,509.75   11. $3,360; $1,848
12. $4,140; $2,070   13. $1,620/$27,000 = .06 = 6%
14. 5%   15. 5 1/2%   16. 4%   17. 5%   18. 7%
19. $4,600/.05 = $92,000   20. $164,000
21. $108,000   22. $86,000   23. $196,000   24. $112,000
25. .07 x .55 = .0385   26. $50,000 x .06 = $3,000
    .0385 x $82,000 = $3,157 $3,000 x .2 = $600
                                      $3,000 - $600 = $2,400
                                      $2,400 x .5 = $1,200
27. $2,700/.06 = $45,000   28. $6,160/$88,000 = .07 = 7%
29. 100% - 6% = 94%   30. 2,350 x $25.50 = $59,925
    $49,000/.94 = $52,127.66
31. 100%/25 = 4% rate of return of capital
    4% + 10% = 14% total required rate of return
    $4,000/.14 = $28,571.43 estimated value of the property
32. (a) (35 x 60) - (5 x 10) = 2,050 sq. ft.
     (b) (40 x 60) - (10 x 8) - (5 x 5) = 2,295 sq. ft.

Learning Unit 15.2

Elements of Cost

in a Closing

1. ($63,000/1,000) x $5.30 = $333.90   2. $403.20; $578.20
    $333.90 + $125.00 = $458.90
3. $260.40; $410.40   4. $188.50; $488.50
5. $319.20; $544.20   6. $283.20; $483.20
7. $65,000 x .01 = $650   8. $2,100
9. $590   10. $710
11. $1,980   12. $1,480
13. 1/2 ÷ 1/8 = 4   14. ($52,000 ÷ 1,000) x $6 = $312
    $32,000 x .04 = $1,280
15. $44,000 x .01 = $440
    $440 + $75 = $515

Learning Unit 15.3

Real Estate Taxes

1. $50,000 x .65 = $32,500   2. $76,000; $646
    ($32,500 ÷ 100) x $1.45 = $471.25
3. $4,800; $228   4. $16,100; $515.20   5. $71,250; $997.50
6. $37,200; $353.40   7. $62,400; $686.40   8. $12,250; $349.13
9. $80,000 x .6 = $48,000   10. $42,630; $315.89
    ($48,000 ÷ 1,000) x $9.72 = $466.56
11. $27,600; $368.46   12. $15,000; $232.20   13. $54,000; $345.06
14. $20,800; $355.68   15. $57,000; $498.18   16. $88,200; $992.25

17. $450,000 x .75 = $337,500
    ($337,500 ÷ 1,000) x $6.42 = $2,166.75
18. $55,000 x .45 = $24,750
    $1.92 + $.65 + $.14 = $2.71
    ($24,750 ÷ 100) x $2.71 = $670.73
19. $68,000 x .4 = $27,200
    ($27,200 ÷ 100) x $4.22 = $1,147.84
    $1,147.84 x .56 = $642.79
20. ($40,000/100) x $3.15 = $1,260
    $375 x 12 = $4,500
    $4,500 - ($1,260 + $2,240) = $1,000

Learning Unit 15.4

Percentage Leases

1. $250,000 x .06 = $15,000
   $225 x 12 = $2,700
   $15,000 + $2,700 = $17,700
2. $300,000 x .04 = $12,000
   $350 x 12 = $4,200
   $12,000 + $4,200 = $16,200
   $16,200 ÷ 12 = $1,350
3. $300,000 x .05 = $15,000
   $275 x 12 = $3,300
   $15,000 + $3,300 = $18,300
4. $250,000 x .08 = $20,000
   $200 x 12 = $2,400
   $20,000 + $2,400 = $22,400
5. $250 x 12 = $3,000
   $19,000 - $3,000 = $16,000
   $16,000 ÷ $400,000 = .04 = 4%
6. $18,000 ÷ $150,000 = .12 = 12%
7. $175 x 12 = $2,100
   $10,850 - $2,100 = $8,750
   $8,750 ÷ $250,000 = .035 = 3.5%
8. $150 x 12 = $1,800
   $10,200 - $1,800 = $8,400
   $8,400 ÷ $120,000 = .07 = 7%

Chapter 15
Self-Evaluation

1. $56,400 x .06 = $3,384
2. $15,500 x .1 = $1,550
   $1,550 x .6 = $930
3. $2,678 ÷ $48,700 = .054989733 = .055 = 5.5%
4. $8,120 ÷ .05 = $162,400
5. 2,050 x $27.50 = $56,375
6. 100% - 6% = 94%
   $56,900 ÷ .94 = $60,531.91
7. ($39,000 ÷ 1,000) x $6.25 = $243.75
   $243.75 + $125 = $368.75
8. $73,000 x .01 = $730
   $730 + $75 = $805
9. 5/8% = 5 points (one mortgage discount point required to make up for
   each 1/8% interest rate loss)

10. $72,700 x .65 = $47,255
     ($47,255 ÷ 100) x $2.95 = $1,394.02
11. $235,000 x .4 = $94,000
     ($94,000 ÷ 100) x $3.45 = $3,243
12. $7,500 x .04 = $300
     $300 + $125 = $425

Chapter 16

The Mathematics of Insurance

A.   Purpose

This chapter explains various insurance terms, such as policy, premium, indemnity, risk, coinsurance, beneficiary, and liability. The chapter also
shows how to distinguish between and compute the cost of various automobile
coverages and how to compute the premium on a fire insurance policy and the
short-rate premium if the policy is cancelled at the request of the insured.
The method for computing the amount of indemnity for a fire loss when a coinsurance clause is involved is explained. The three basic types of life insurance policies are described, as well as the methods for computing the
premium for these coverages on an annual, semiannual, quarterly, and monthly
basis.

B.   Comments

 1. Several terms presented in this chapter are not familiar to many stu-
     dents and should be explained by the instructor.
 2. The procedure for computing the amount of indemnity for a fire loss
     when a coinsurance clause is involved should be emphasized.

C.   Solutions

Learning Unit 16.1

Automobile Insurance

 1. $20,000; $4,000   2. $16,000; $5,000   3. $20,000; $8,000
 4. $31,000; $10,000   5. $7,000; $25,000   6. $49,000; $17,000

7. $71   8. $69   9. $68   10. $87
11. $96 x 1.08 = $103.68   12. $39 x 1.38 = $53.82
13. $100 x 1.05 = $105   14. $86 x 1.29 = $110.94
15. $42   16. $40   17. $47   18. $43   19. $25
20. $45   21. $54   22. $34   23. $169   24. $117
25. $326 x 1.57 = $511.82   26. $164 x .47 = $77.08
27. $89 x 1.33 = $118.37   28. $127 x 1.57 = $199.39
29. $428   30. $272 x 1.33 = $361.76
31. $937 - $100 = $837   32. $47 + $60 = $107
33. $57 x 1.84 = $104.88   34. $326 x 1.57 = $511.82
     $76 x 1.08 = $82.08 $112 x 1.57 = 175.84
     $104.88 + $82.08 = $186.96 $335.98

Learning Unit 16.2

Fire Insurance

1. ($50,000 ÷ 100) x $.162 = $81.00
2. $262.39   3. $260.11   4. $192.72
5. $386.60   6. $38.64   7. $653.40
8. ($19,000 ÷ 100) x $.334 = $63.46   9. $195; $37.05
    $63.46 x .72 = $45.69
10. $198.72; $103.33   11. $241.86; $154.79
12. $162.00; $50.22   13. $144.90; $31.88
14. $49,000 x .8 = $39,200 < $40,000
     Amount of indemnity = Property loss = $15,000
15. $23,000
16. $28,000 ÷ ($33,000 x .9) x $7,000 = $6,599.33
17. $18,000   18. $5,500   19. $4,401.41
20. $8,437.50   21. $39,187.57
22. $168 x .20 = $33.60   23. 400 x $.165 = $66
     $168 - $33.60 = $134.40 $66 x 2.7 = $178.20
24. 1,200 x $.224 = $268.80 annual premium
     $268.80 x 4.4 = $1,182.72 five-year premium
     ($268.80 x 5) - $1,182.72 = $161.28 savings over five years
     $161.28 ÷ 5 = $32.26 annual savings
25. $60,000 ÷ ($78,000 x .80) x $22,000 = $21,153.85
26. $90,000 ÷ ($120,000 x .80) x $22,000 = $20,625

Learning Unit 16.3

Life Insurance

1. $14.30   2. $33.07   3. $37.24
4. $12.07   5. $2.37   6. $2.58
7. ($100,000 ÷ $1,000) x $2.88 = $288   8. $14.30; $357.50
9. $21.42; $535.50   10. $36.41; $910.25   11. $25.91; $259.10
12. $2.58; $129.00   13. $33.07; $496.05   14. $38.73; $387.30
15. ($10,000 ÷ $1,000) x $2.88 = $28.80 annual premium
     $28.80 x .51 = $14.69 semiannual premium
     $28.80 x .26 = $7.49 quarterly premium
     $28.80 x .09 = $2.59 monthly premium
16. $143; $72.93; $37.18; $12.87
17. $214.20; $109.24; $55.69; $19.28
18. $364.10; $185.69; $94.67; $32.77
19. ($20,000 ÷ $1,000) x $10.13 = $202.60 annual premium
     $202.60 x .26 = $52.676 quarterly premium
     (4 x $52.676) - $202.60 = $8.10 annual savings
20. $180 ÷ $2.58 = 69.767 x 1,000 = $69,767, or $70,000

21. ($100,000 ÷ $1,000) x $19.55 = $1,955
22. ($50,000 ÷ $1,000) x $5.30 = $265

Chapter 16
Self-Evaluation

1. ($56,000 ÷ 100) x $.635 = $355.60
2. ($235,000 ÷ 100) x $.93 = $2,185.50
    $2,185.50 x .4 = $874.20
3. $52,000 ÷ ($84,000 x .8) x $21,000 = $16,250
4. ($25,000 ÷ $1,000) x $16.44 = $411 annual premium
    $411 x .09 = $36.99 monthly premium
5. ($25,000 ÷ $1,000) x $35.18 = $879.50 annual premium
    $879.50 x .26 = $228.67 quarterly premium
6. $20,000 is the maximum limit for bodily injury on the auto policy.

Chapter 17

Transportation

A.   Purpose

This chapter explains how to compute transportation costs, taking into consideration the basic weight classifications, the break point between rate classifications, and ancillary costs.

B.   Comments

1. Transportation costs are assigned on the basis of weight classification and distance.
2. Savings in transportation costs can be affected by applying the concepts of break point and combined shipment.
3. It is the responsibility of the person doing the shipping, not the transportation company, to determine the most efficient method of shipping.
4. Mention should be made of the fact that volume charging rather than weight rates is beginning to emerge as a basis for setting transportation rates.

C.   Solutions

Learning Unit 17.1

Weights and Rates

1. $2{,}700 \div 100 \times \$1.24 = \$33.48$
2. \$86.19   3. \$244.13   4. \$313.63
5. \$117.05   6. \$208.73   7. \$90.75
8. \$307.50   9. \$353.72   10. \$644.64

11. 8,600 ÷ 100 x $1.68 = $144.48
12. $218.79   13. $33.60 (minimum charge)   14. $369.74
15. $133.06   16. $467.48   17. $267.90
18. $446.88   19. $462.17   20. $353.43
21. (23,200 ÷ 100) x $1.27 = $294.64
22. (27,840 + 17,650 + 4,520) ÷ 2,000 x $18 = $450.09
23. 70,000 ÷ 2,240 x $16 = $500.00

Learning Unit 17.2

Break Point and

Ancillary Costs

1. $\frac{5,000 \text{ x } (\$1.97 \div 100)}{\$2.10 \div 100} = \frac{98.5}{.021} = 4,690$ pounds

2. 13,857   3.   23,214   4.   35,266
5. 4,000 ÷ 100 x $1.67 = $66.80 minimum charge

   $\frac{15,000 \text{ x } (\$1.58 \div 100)}{\$1.67 \quad 100} = 14,191$ break point

6. $237.00; 27,151   7. $429.00; 43,006
8. $615.00; 59,837   9. $736.00
10. 28,000 ÷ 2,000 x $23 = $322
    28,000 ÷ 2,000 x $26 =   364
                          $686

11. 56,000 ÷ 2,000 x $22 + $50 = $666

12. 70,000 ÷ 2,000 x $16 = $ 560 (above B-E point)
    80,000 ÷ 2,000 x $19 =   760 (above B-E point)
                          $1,320

13. 150,000 ÷ 2,000 x $13 + 50 = $1,025

14. 80,000 ÷ 2,000 x $16 = $640
    100,000 ÷ 2,000 x $19 = 950 $1,590

    180,000 ÷ 2,000 x $13 + 50 =   -1,220
                                 $ 370 less expensive using combined
                                        shipment

Chapter 17
Self-Evaluation

1. 41,780/2,000 x $18.40 = $384.38
2. 1,916/100 x $.93 = $17.82
3. 76,000/2,240 x $15 = $508.93

4. $\frac{18,000 \text{ x } (\$1.68 \div 100)}{(\$1.82 \div 100)} = 16,524$ pounds

5. 16,000/100 x $.97 = $155.20
    16,000/100 x $.89 =   142.40
                                    $297.60

    32,000/100 x $.80 + $30 =   286.00
                                    $ 11.60 combined

Chapter 18

Business Statistics

A.   Purpose

Many business people are involved on a daily basis in the use of statistical
information. Success in business often depends to a considerable extent on
the ability to read and accurately interpret statistical data. This chapter
explains (1) some of the forms in which data are presented to management for
analysis, and (2) the measures of central tendency useful in business
decision-making.

B.   Comments

1. The fact that measures of central tendency for grouped data are at
    best approximations should be emphasized.
2. Much more sophisticated formulae for finding the median and mean for
    grouped data are available for those seeking a more mathematical
    approach.

C.   Solutions

Learning Unit 18.1

Measures of

Central Tendency

1. 219 + 227 + 234 + 238 + 242 + 246 + 246 + 254 = 1,906
    (a) mean = 1,906/8 = 238.25
    (b) median = (238 + 242)/2 = 480/2 = 240
    (c) mode = 246

2. 59 + 62 + 68 + 71 + 71 + 74 + 78 + 83 + 87 + 90 + 91 + 93 = 927
   (a) mean = 927/12 = 77.25
   (b) median = (74 + 78)/2 = 152/2 = 76
   (c) mode = 71
3. $7,000 + 9,000 + 11,000 + 14,000 + 24,000 = $65,000
   (a) mean = $65,000/5 = $13,000
   (b) median = $11,000
   (c) median
4. $143 + 214 + 264 + 287 + 297 = $1,205
   (a) mean = $1,205/5 = $241
   (b) median = $264
5. 84 + 86 + 90 + 96 = 356; 356/4 = 89
6. 174 + 187 + 197 = 558; 558/3 = 186
7. 14 + 16 + 18 + 21 + 23 + 23 + 29 = 144
   (a) mean = 144/7 = 20.57 (rounded)
   (b) median = 21
   (c) mode = 23
8. 528/11 = 48

Learning Unit 18.2

Grouped Data

1.

C.I.	Tally	f	x	f · x
0 - 49	ʜɪ III	8	25	200
50 - 99	ʜɪ I	6	75	450
100 - 149	ʜɪ	5	125	625
150 - 199	ʜɪ	5	175	875
		$\Sigma f = 24$		$\Sigma f \cdot x$ 2,150

(a) $\bar{x} = (\Sigma f \cdot x)/\Sigma f = 2,150/24 = 89.58$
(b) M = 50 + (12 - 8)/6 · 50
    M = 66.67 or 66 2/3
(c) Modal class = 0 - 49

2.

C.I.	Tally	f	Midpoint x	f · x
1 - 3	ʜɪ ʜɪ ʜɪ	15	2.5	37.5
4 - 6	ʜɪ ʜɪ II	12	5.5	66.0
7 - 9	ʜɪ ʜɪ II	12	8.5	102.0
10 - 12	I	1	11.5	11.5
		$\Sigma f = 40$		$\Sigma f \cdot x = 217.0$

(a) $\bar{x} = (\Sigma f \cdot x)/\Sigma f = 217/40 = 5.425$
(b) $M = CI_L + \dfrac{\Sigma f/2 - \Sigma f_L}{f_{MC}} \cdot I$

    M = 4 + (20 - 15)/12 · 3
    M = 5.25
(c) Modal class = 1 - 3

3.

C.I.	f	x	f · x
40 – 49	1	45	45
50 – 59	3	55	165
60 – 69	7	65	455
70 – 79	9	75	675
80 – 89	9	85	765
90 – 99	4	95	380
	$\Sigma f = 33$		$\Sigma f \cdot x = 2{,}485$

(a) $\bar{x} = (\Sigma f \cdot x)/\Sigma f = 2{,}485/33 = 75.3$

(b) $M = CI_L + \dfrac{(\Sigma f/2 - \Sigma f_L)}{fMC} \cdot I$

$M = 70 + (16.5 - 11)/9 \times 10$

$M = 70 + 55/9$

$M = 70 + 6.11 = 76.11$

(c) Modal class = Bimodal 70 - 79 and 80 - 89

4.

C.I.	f	x	f · x
$ 8,000 – 11,999	27	$10,000	$ 270,000
12,000 – 15,999	32	14,000	448,000
16,000 – 19,999	21	18,000	378,000
20,000 – 23,999	12	22,000	264,000
24,000 – 27,999	9	26,000	234,000
28,000 – 31,999	6	30,000	180,000
	$\Sigma f = 107$		$\Sigma f \cdot x = \$1{,}774{,}000$

(a) $\bar{x} = (\Sigma f \cdot x)/\Sigma f = 1{,}774{,}000/107 = \$16{,}579.44$

(b) $M = CI_L + \dfrac{(\Sigma f/2 - \Sigma f_L)}{fMC} \cdot I$

$M = \$12{,}000 + (53.5 - 27)/32 \times \$4{,}000$

$M = \$12{,}000 + \$3{,}312.50$

$M = \$15{,}312.50$

(c) Modal class = $12,000 - $15,999

5.

C.I.	f	x (000's)	f · x (000's)
10 – 69	79	40	3,160
70 – 129	121	100	12,100
130 – 189	32	160	5,120
	$\Sigma f = 232$		$\Sigma f \cdot x = 20{,}380$

(a) $\bar{x} = 20{,}380{,}000/232 = 87{,}845$

(b) $M = 70{,}000 + (126 - 79)/121 \times 60{,}000$

$M = 93{,}306$

(c) Modal class = 70 - 129

Learning Unit 18.3

Presentation of

Statistical Data

1.   COMPARISON OF SALES AND COST OF GOODS SOLD

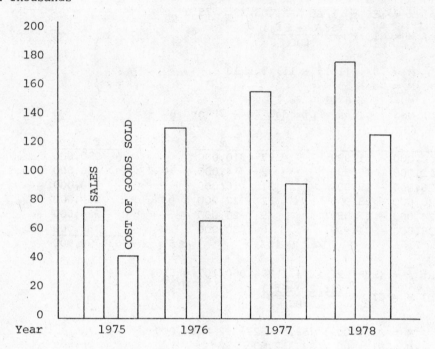

2.   SELLING PRICE AND COST OF WIDGETS

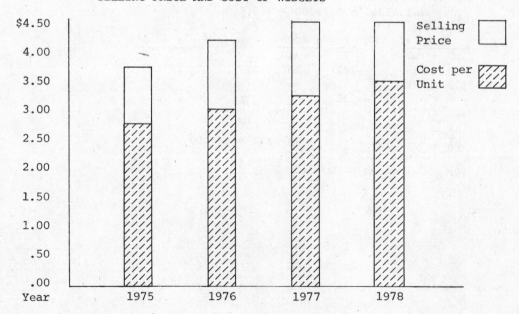

3. EMPLOYEE TURNOVER

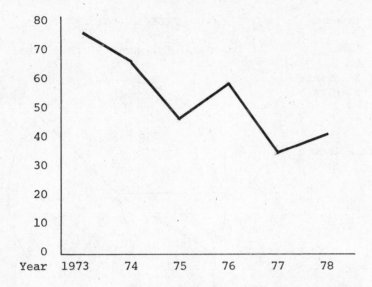

4. SHARES TRADED ON REGISTERED EXCHANGES

1966   1976

3.2 Billion Shares = 100%   7 Billion Shares = 100%

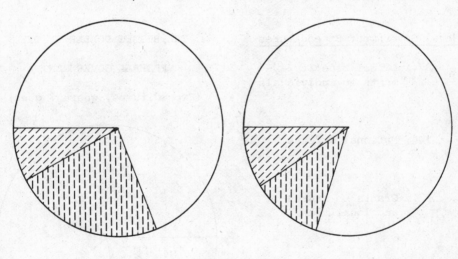

☐ New York Stock Exchange

▦ American Stock Exchange

▨ Other Stock Exchanges

5. <u>Federal Government Receipts</u>

       38¢, Income taxes

       28¢, Social Insurance
           Receipts (FICA)

       13¢, Corporate income
           taxes

       12¢, Borrowing

        9¢, Other

THE BUDGET DOLLAR OF THE

FEDERAL GOVERNMENT

(Receipts, where $ comes from)

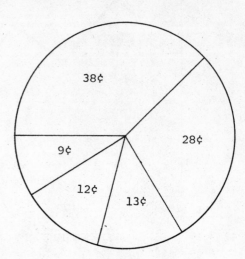

<u>Federal Government Expenditures</u>

       37¢, Direct benefit pay-
           ments to individuals

       24¢, National defense

       17¢, Grants to states
           and localities

       14¢, Other federal
           operations

        8¢, Interest

THE BUDGET DOLLAR OF THE

FEDERAL GOVERNMENT

(Expenditures, where $ goes)

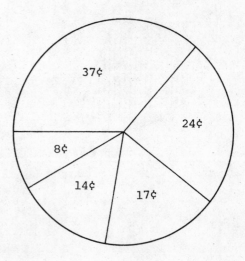

6. EQUIVALENT YIELDS FOR TAXABLE AND NONTAXABLE BONDS AT SELECTED LEVELS

OF TAXABLE INCOME

Selected Taxable Incomes (joint return)	Tax Bracket (marginal tax rate)	Equivalent Taxable Yields If Tax Exempt Yield Is 7%
$ 20,000 - $ 24,000	32%	10.29%
$ 32,000 - $ 36,000	42%	12.07%
$ 44,000 - $ 52,000	50%	14.00%
$ 76,000 - $ 88,000	58%	16.67%
$120,000 - $140,000	64%	19.44%

Chapter 18
Self-Evaluation

1. (a) 934/12 = 77.83
    (b) 77 + 82 = 159; 159/2 = 79.5
    (c) 71 & 82, both occur twice
2. (a) 1,268/88 = 14.41
    (b) $\underline{m}$ = 11 + (44 - 19)/38 x 5; $\underline{m}$ = 11 + 3.29; $\underline{m}$ = 14.29
    (c) Modal class = 11 - 15

3.

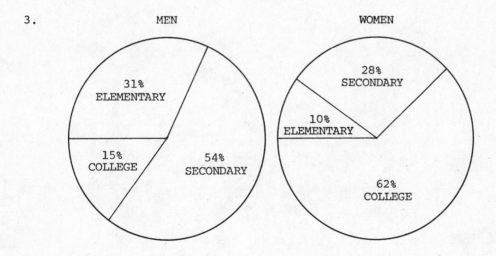

4.

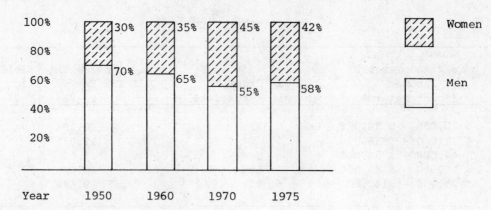

Test Bank

Chapter 1

Learning Unit 1.1

1. Write the following number in words: 264
2. Write the following number in words: 1,898
3. Express the following number in figures: twenty-eight thousand
4. Express the following number in figures: three thousand eight hundred three
5. Name the place position of the zero in the following number: 80,462
6. Name the place position of the five in the following number: 36,452,949
7. What digit in 12,345,789 has the millions value?
8. What digit in 12,345,789 has the ten-thousands value?
9. Write the following decimal number as it would be expressed in words: .93
10. Write the following decimal number as it would be expressed in words: .157

Learning Unit 1.2

11. Round the following number to hundredths: .763
12. Round the following number to hundredths: .51499
13. Round the following number to hundredths: .00761
14. The gas bill for heating a building was calculated to be $186.51792. What was the billing amount?
15. If the annual depreciation on a front-end loader was $719.8254, how much was recorded, to the nearest dollar, for depreciation on the machine?

Learning Unit 1.3

16. Add: 17. Add:
    838   501
    227   926
    194   339
    605   487

18. Add the following numbers by obtaining subtotals and summing them:
    702
    549
    832 _____ subtotal
    931
    361
    440 _____ subtotal
    913
    571
    663 _____ subtotal
               sum

19. Add the following numbers by obtaining subtotals and summing them:
    809
    746
    555 _____ subtotal
    912
    386
    412 _____ subtotal
    111
    397
    304 _____ subtotal
               sum

20. Subtract: 21. Subtract:
    862   3,479
   -455   -2,560

22. During the week of July 17, the Hampton Manufacturing Company produced the following item. What was the total produced during this period?

Article	M	T	W	T	F	Total
Slide Trays	386	416	550	372	418	_____

23. Determine the total weekly sales for the following item at the Summit Wholesale Company.

Model #	M	T	W	T	F	Total
A 140	$967	$1,480	$1,026	$828	$1,512	_____

Learning Unit 1.4

24. Multiply: 25. Multiply:
    2,367   16,474
    x 253   x 627

26. Divide: 27. Divide:
    4,792/62   1,967/43

28. Twenty-one people were enrolled in a French cooking class at a community college. The fee was $36 for each person. How much was collected for the class?
29. On a recent trip, Bonnie drove 2,604 miles in six days. How many miles per day did she average?
30. Bill Reeves restores classic automobiles. He recently paid $315 for a 1957 Chevrolet. How much did he receive for the automobile if he sold it for four times the cost?
31. A farmer sells bales of hay for $4 each. If his sales were $624 last week, how many bales did he sell?

Learning Unit 1.5

32. Add:
    .112
    176.3
    46.7
    19.32
    1.6
    47.32

33. Add:
    .4719
    81.35
    716
    1.0091
    15.77
    847.26

34. Subtract:
    $182.76
    - 49.88

35. Subtract:
    126.60
    -84.76

36. During the past month Barb Russell made deposits of $176.24, $324.09, $287.55, and $87.96. What was the total amount deposited?
37. If a metric measurement socket wrench set priced at $27.98 was placed on sale for $20.47, how much was the decrease in price?
38. Bob Key had the following meal at a cafeteria: tossed salad, $.60; grilled steak, $1.19; beans, $.38; pie, $.47. How much change did he receive if he paid for the meal with a $10 bill?

Learning Unit 1.6

39. Multiply:
    $4.25
    x.64

40. Multiply:
    19.26
    x.147

41. Divide and round the quotient to hundredths: 73/4.9
42. Divide and round the quotient to thousandths: 23.74/.807
43. Use shortcut procedures in working the following problem:
     84
    x10
44. Use shortcut procedures in working the following problem:
    820/100 =
45. Use shortcut procedures in working the following problem:
    114
    x30
46. Use shortcut procedures in working the following problem:
    22.5/25 =
47. Rope sells for 28¢ a foot. How many feet can be bought for $36.96?
48. If Sylvia Morris's automobile gets 14.7 miles to the gallon, how many gallons will she need to make a trip of 1,323 miles?
49. If carpeting sells for $15.86 a square yard, how much will 14.75 square yards cost?

Chapter 2

Learning Unit 2.1

1. Reduce to lowest terms: 35/63
2. Reduce to lowest terms: 174/522
3. Supply the missing numerator: 9/16 = __/96
4. Supply the missing numerator: 2/15 = __/60

Learning Unit 2.2

5. Change to a mixed number: 33/7
6. Change to a mixed number: 58/11
7. Change to an improper fraction: 4 5/6
8. Change to an improper fraction: 8 5/9
9. Convert to a decimal: 3/8
10. Convert to a decimal: 2/7
11. Convert to a fraction: .19
12. Convert to a fraction: .6

Learning Unit 2.3

13. Add: 3/4 + 4/9 + 5/12
14. Add: 14 5/7 + 3 5/10 + 22 1/5
15. Subtract: 19/21 - 5/6
16. Subtract: 7/9 - 2/15
17. Jill St. Clair must set aside 1/5 of her salary to pay for rent and utilities and 1/12 to pay for care and purchase of clothing. What fractional portion does she spend for her living quarters and clothing?
18. Ron's Rags recently received an order of clothing: 4/9 of the items was women's sportswear, 1/4 was better dresses, and the remainder was formal wear. What fractional portion of the order was the formal wear?
19. Erek's desk top is 1 3/16 inches thick. The legs on the desk are 27 7/8 inches high. How far is the top writing surface of Erek's desk from the floor?

Learning Unit 2.4

20. Multiply: 2/7 by 3/5
21. Multiply: 11/12 by 4/9
22. Multiply: 7/12 x 5/14 x 9/10
23. Multiply: 2/5 x 15/32 x 8/11
24. Multiply: 17 4/5 by 1 2/3
25. Multiply: 8 1/10 by 7 4/9
26. Divide: 4/7 by 8/15
27. Divide: 30 by 15/16
28. Divide: 6 7/8 by 14 3/4
29. Divide: 5 5/6 by 7 6/7
30. Of 900 coats placed on sale, the merchant sold 1/5 of them the first day. How many coats were sold?
31. If the zoning restrictions require 3/7 of an acre for a residential lot, how many lots are contained in 45 acres?
32. A recipe that serves four uses 1 3/4 pounds of ground meat. How many pounds of ground meat are needed to serve 48 people?

Chapter 3

Learning Unit 3.1

1. Change to a decimal: 37.61%
2. Change to a decimal: 3/4 %
3. Change to a percent: 2.63
4. Change to a percent: .035
5. Change to a fraction: 75%
6. Change to a fraction: 39%
7. Change to a percent: 1/8
8. Change to a percent: 2/3

Learning Unit 3.2

Solve for the variable.

9. $17 + a = 35$ 10. $C + 5 = 16$
11. $B - 3 = 9$ 12. $7 - M = 2$
13. $5R = 15$ 14. $3P = 7$
15. $A/3 = 7$ 16. $A/\frac{1}{2} = 10$

Learning Unit 3.3

17. Determine the part: Base = $375, Rate = 12%
18. Determine the part: Base = $6.45, Rate = 7 1/5%
19. Determine the base, rounding to the nearest cent.
    Portion = $2.67, Rate = 3.5%
20. Determine the base, rounding to the nearest cent.
    Portion = 125.21, Rate = 8 3/8%
21. Determine the rate, rounding to the nearest whole percent.
    Base = $750, Portion = $60
22. Determine the rate, rounding to the nearest whole percent.
    Base = $865, Portion = $95
23. A refrigerator costing $865 requires a down payment of 15%. Find the amount of the down payment.
24. How much is the sales tax on a purchase of $82.96 if the tax rate is 6%?
25. A department store charges 80% of its rental cost to selling expense. How much will be charged to selling expense if the monthly rent is $1,700?
26. What is the rate of discount if a camera priced at $470 is sold for $329?
27. The K-Tex Manufacturing Company produced 27,400 trailers last year and 22,600 this year. The production this year is what percentage of the number of trailers produced last year?
28. If a salesperson received $2,550 commission from a house that sold for $42,500, what rate of commission was paid?
29. A savings account yielding a 6 1/2% rate paid $51.05 interest last year. How much was deposited in the account?
30. Tracey budgeted 11% of her take-home pay for savings. If she deposited $101.64 in her savings account this month, how much was her take-home pay?

Chapter 4

Learning Unit 4.1

1. Determine the trade price.
    List price, $120; Discount rate, 30%
2. Determine the trade price.
    List price, $720; Discount rate, 18%
3. Find the single discount equal to the following discounts:
    30%, 20%, 10%
4. Find the single discount equal to the following discounts:
    25%, 15%, 10%
5. Find the trade price.
    List price, $118.70; Chain discount, 20%, 10%
6. Find the trade price.
    List price, $87.40; Chain discount, 25%, 15%
7. The list price of an invoice has trade discounts of 20% and 10%. What
    amount is necessary to pay the $196.35 invoice?
8. Two wholesalers bid on an order of rug shampoo. Which of the following
    is the lower bid? How much less is it? Bid A, $7,700, 40% and 10% off;
    Bid B, $7,500, 30% and 20% off
9. Goods priced at $2,360 were bought at 15% and 10% off. If the freight
    charges (included in the invoice) are $47.60, what are the trade price
    and the billing price?

Learning Unit 4.2

10. Find the amount of cash discount and payment.
    Invoice, $187.65; Cash discount, 2/10, n/30
11. Find the amount of cash discount and payment.
    Invoice, $417.65; Cash discount, 3/20, n/90
12. What are the last days of the discount period and credit period?
    Date of invoice, May 19; Terms, 1/20, n/90
13. What are the last days of the discount period and credit period?
    Date of invoice, December 6; Terms, 3/15, n/60
14. What are the cash discount and amount of payment?
    Invoice, $176.40; Returned goods, $25; Freight charges, $11.40;
    Terms, 2/10, n/30
15. What are the cash discount and amount of payment?
    Invoice, $136.47; Returned goods, $30.00; Freight charges, $5.00;
    Terms, 3/10, n/60
16. What are the cash discount and amount of payment?
    Invoice date, January 26; Invoice, $128.67; Terms, 2/10, n/30;
    Date of payment, February 5
17. What are the cash discount and amount of payment?
    Invoice date, June 7; Invoice, $362.50; Terms, 2/10 EOM; Returned
    goods, $17.40; Date of payment, July 10
18. Find the credit for the following partial payment and the amount out-
    standing after the partial payment.
    Invoice, $748.50; Terms, 2/10, n/30; Partial payment, $245
19. Find the credit for the following partial payment and the amount out-
    standing after the partial payment.
    Invoice, $1,260.73; Terms, 3/15, n/120; Partial payment, $606.25
20. The $900 list price of an invoice dated June 25 has trade discounts of
    15% and 10% and terms of 2/15, n/60. What amount is necessary to pay
    the invoice on July 8?

21. An invoice dated February 3 for $426.82 had terms of 2/20, n/60. The goods were inspected and goods worth $37.26 were returned as defective. If the invoice amount includes freight charges of $12.40, what amount is paid if payment is made on February 23?

22. A partial payment of $320 was made on a $750 invoice. If the terms were 4/10, n/60, how much credit was received for the partial payment? How much is still outstanding?

88

Chapter 5

Learning Unit 5.1

1. Determine the retail price for the following 31-day striking clock if the cost is $78 and the dollar markon is $51.
2. Determine the retail price for a silver pitcher that costs $22.40 if the markon is 48 percent of cost.
3. Determine the retail price for a silver bud vase that costs $22.70 if the markon is 38 percent of cost.
4. Determine the cost of a peanut machine that has a retail price of $14.74 if the markon is 53 percent of cost.
5. Determine the cost of a bookstand that has a retail price of $51.00 if the markon is 20 percent of cost.
6. Determine the markon percent on cost for a pair of shears that costs $7.60 and retails for $9.53.
7. Determine the markon percent on cost for a pair of rain boots that costs $13.50 and retails for $19.98.
8. Determine the retail price of a chrome tray that costs $6.92 if the markon is 46 percent of retail.
9. Determine the retail price of a silver pitcher that costs $20.90 if the markon is 48 percent of retail.
10. Determine the markon percent on retail for a pair of scissors that costs $4.30 and retails for $5.50.
11. Determine the markon percent on retail for a pair of rain boots that costs $13.50 and retails for $19.98.
12. A dealer bought a chair from a manufacturer for $90. At what price must the chair retail to maintain a markon of 25 percent of retail?
13. A coffee pot was bought for $18.75. A retail price of $24.95 was advertised. What percent of markon on the retail price does this represent?
14. A student desk was sold for $146.60. What was the cost of the desk if the markon was 40 percent of cost?

Learning Unit 5.2

15. A grocer bought 200 pounds of tomatoes at $.25 a pound. It is expected that 20% of the tomatoes will not be sold. What price per pound should be charged in order to make 30% on cost for the total purchase?
16. A local snow cone stand buys 500 pounds of ice each day at a cost of $25 and experiences a loss of 20% due to melting. Total syrup and cup expense for an average day is $45. What is the price of a snow cone if each cone consists of 16 ounces of ice and a markon of 40% of cost is used?

Learning Unit 5.3

17. What is the new retail price of the following stereo speaker if the original price was $99.95 and the markdown is $15.60?
18. A clock priced to sell at $75.00 has been reduced to $40.00. Determine the percent of markdown based on the original retail price.
19. A mirror priced to sell at $50.15 is reduced to $38.58. Determine the percent of markdown based on the original retail price.
20. A two-drawer file cabinet priced to sell at $40.35 is reduced to $26.90. Determine the percent of markdown based on the new retail price.

21. A hand-held calculator priced to sell at $52.70 is reduced to $37.64. Determine the percent of markdown based on the new retail price.
22. A stopwatch priced at $31.50 is reduced 14 percent. Determine the new retail price when the percent of markdown is based on the original retail price.
23. A book priced at $12.99 is to be reduced 25 percent. Determine the new retail price when the percent of markdown is based on the original retail price.
24. A desk set priced at $87.00 is to be reduced 40 percent. Determine the new retail price when the percent of markdown is based on the new retail price.
25. A putter priced at $14.25 is reduced 30 percent. Determine the new retail price when the percent of markdown is based on the new retail price.
26. A sewing machine priced at $194.95 is advertised at 23 percent off the regular price. Find the sale price of the sewing machine.
27. A package of razor blades priced at $2.97 is advertised at $1.88. Find the percent of markdown on the new price.

Chapter 6

Learning Unit 6.1

1. Determine the monthly earnings of an employee who earns $288 a week.
2. Determine the semimonthly earnings of an employee who earns $11,688 a year.
3. Determine the weekly salary of an employee who earns $1,040 a month.
4. Determine the weekly earnings of an employee who earns $7.75 an hour and worked 46 hours last week. Calculate time and a half for work in excess of 40 hours.
5. Determine the weekly earnings of an employee who earns $9.45 an hour and worked 43 hours last week. Calculate time and a half for hours worked in excess of 40.
6. Determine the earnings of an employee who worked 42 hours and assembled 43 weed trimmers last week. The company pays $2.80 an hour plus $4.00 for each trimmer assembled.
7. Determine the earnings of an employee who worked 45 1/2 hours last week and assembled 39 week trimmers. The company pays $2.80 an hour plus $4.00 for each trimmer assembled.
8. Determine the earnings of an employee who sold $5,700 last week and receives commissions of 5 percent on the first $4,000 and 7 percent on the remainder.
9. Determine the earnings of an employee who sold $8,250 last week and receives a salary of $100 plus commissions of 3 percent on the first $5,000 and 5 percent on the remainder.

Learning Unit 6.2

10. Jim is married, claims four exemptions, and earns a monthly salary of $1,600. Calculate the F.I.C.A. tax, income tax, and take-home pay for this month's pay check. (Use the wage bracket method.)
11. Maria is married, claims two exemptions, and is paid $4.80 an hour plus time and a half for overtime over 40 hours a week. Last week she worked 47 1/2 hours. Determine her take-home pay for the week if she deducts F.I.C.A., income tax, and $10 a week for insurance. (Use the percentage method.)

Chapter 7

Learning Unit 7.1

1. A truck was purchased for $9,800. The estimated useful life of the truck is four years with a trade-in value of $1,000. What is the annual depreciation using the straight-line method of computing depreciation?
2. The estimated life of a machine that was purchased for $25,000 is ten years with a residual value of $5,000. What is the annual depreciation using the straight-line method of computing depreciation?
3. A company purchased a machine for $13,000. The transportation charges on the machine were $325. Insurance charges paid by the company while the machine was in transit were $37. What was the total cost of the machine?
4. A real estate broker purchased an automobile for $9,600. The broker plans to trade the car in at the end of three years and expects a trade-in value of $3,600 at that time. (a) Using the straight-line method of computing depreciation, how much depreciation will occur each year? (b) What is the book value at the end of the first year?

Learning Unit 7.2

5. A truck was purchased for $9,800. The estimated useful life of the truck is 100,000 miles with a trade-in value of $1,000. What is the annual depreciation for a year in which the truck was driven 28,000 miles? Use the units of productive capacity method of computing depreciation.
6. A machine was purchased for $135,000. The productive capacity of the machine is estimated to be 20,000 hours with a trade-in value of $9,000. What is the annual depreciation for a year in which the machine was used 2,230 hours? Use the units of productive capacity method of computing depreciation.

Learning Unit 7.3

7. (a) What is the sum-of-the-years-digits depreciation fraction for the first year on an asset that has a useful life of six years? (b) For the third year?
8. An office machine was purchased for $14,016. The estimated life of the machine is eight years with a residual value of $2,400. Using the sum-of-the-years-digits depreciation method, determine (a) the first year depreciation and (b) the book value at the end of the first year.
9. An asset that cost $42,200 has an estimated life of seven years and an estimated residual value of $7,000. The asset was purchased August 18 of the current year. Compute the depreciation for the current year using the sum-of-the-years-digits depreciation method.

Learning Unit 7.4

10. What is the annual double-declining balance depreciation rate for an asset with an estimated life of eight years?
11. An office machine was purchased for $14,016. The estimated life of the machine is eight years with a residual value of $2,400. Using the double-declining balance depreciation method, determine (a) the first year depreciation and (b) the book value at the end of the first year.

12. An asset that cost $42,200 has an estimated life of seven years and an estimated residual value of $7,000. The asset was purchased August 18 of the current year. Compute the depreciation for the current year using the double-declining balance depreciation method.

Chapter 8

Learning Unit 8.1

1. A company maintains a stock of item B-49. There were 9 units of this
    item in the company's ending inventory. Determine the cost that the
    company should assign to the ending inventory for this item under each
    of the inventory costing methods.

Date	Source	Quantity	Unit Cost
January 1	Inventory	6	$34
February 8	Purchase	10	36
April 6	Purchase	15	37
July 13	Purchase	8	39
October 27	Purchase	7	40

(a) Specific Identification (3 of the units were purchased on February 8;
    2 of the units were purchased on July 13; and 4 of the units were
    purchased on October 27.)
(b) First-in, First-out (FIFO)
(c) Last-in, First-out (LIFO)
(d) Average Cost

2. A company maintains a stock of item G-49. There were 6 units in the
    ending inventory. What cost should the company assign to the inventory
    for the 6 units of this item under each of the inventory costing
    methods?

Date	Source	Quantity	Unit Cost
January 1	Inventory	2 units	$115
March 22	Purchase	30 units	126
May 30	Purchase	20 units	128
July 12	Purchase	20 units	130
August 27	Purchase	10 units	125

(a) Specific Identification (1 unit was purchased March 22; 1 unit was
    purchased July 12; and 4 units were purchased August 27.)
(b) First-in, First out (FIFO)
(c) Last-in, First-out (LIFO)
(d) Average Cost

Learning Unit 8.2

3. The financial records of the Ornee Company contain the following infor-
    mation. Determine the cost of merchandise sold.
    Merchandise Inventory, January 1, 19__ $ 45,000
    Merchandise Inventory, December 31, 19__   47,000

Purchases	$324,000
Transportation Charges on Purchases	15,000
Purchase Returns and Allowances	12,000
Purchase Discounts	6,200

4. The Gourmet Specialty Shop's accounting records contain the following information. Determine the cost of merchandise sold.

Merchandise Inventory, January 1, 19__	$ 32,000
Merchandise Inventory, December 31, 19__	30,000
Purchases	290,000
Transportation Charges on Purchases	13,000
Purchase Returns and Allowances	9,000
Purchase Discounts	5,600

Chapter 9

Learning Unit 9.1

1. Prepare a vertical analysis of the income statement of the Smith Company for 19_1. Use net sales as the base for comparison of the items.

Smith Company
Income Statement
Year Ended December 31, 19_1

	Amount	Percent
Revenue:		
Net Sales	$245,000	100.00
Operating Expenses:		
Cost of Merchandise Sold	122,500	___
Salaries Expense	22,050	___
Wages Expense	39,200	___
Depreciation Expense	7,350	___
Miscellaneous Expense	4,900	___
Total Expenses	$196,000	___
Net Income	49,000	___

2. Prepare a vertical analysis of the balance sheet of the ABC Company. Use total assets as the base for comparison of the items.

ABC Company
Balance Sheet
December 31, 19_1

	Amount	Percent
Assets		
Cash	$ 7,770	___
Accounts Receivable	27,750	___
Supplies	1,110	___
Merchandise Inventory	49,950	___
Equipment (Less Accumulated Depreciation)	24,420	___
Total Assets	$111,000	100.00
Liabilities		
Accounts Payable	25,530	___
Notes Payable	27,750	___
Total Liabilities	$ 53,280	___
Capital		
C. B. Jones, Capital	$ 57,720	
Total Liabilities and Capital	$111,000	100.00

3. Prepare a horizontal analysis of the comparative income statement for The Appliance Center.

The Appliance Center
Comparative Income Statement
Years Ended December 31, 19_1, and December 31, 19_2

	Years Ended December 31		Amount of Increase or (Decrease)	Percent of Increase or (Decrease)
	19_2	19_1		
Revenue:				
Net Sales	$197,000	$177,300	_____	_____
Operating Expenses:				
Cost of Merchandise Sold	$137,000	$123,300	_____	_____
Wages Expense	18,000	17,280	_____	_____
Advertising Expense	7,300	6,789	_____	_____
Miscellaneous Expense	1,000	860	_____	_____
Total Expenses	$163,300	$148,229	_____	_____
Net Income	$ 33,700	$ 29,071	_____	_____

4. Prepare a horizontal analysis of the comparative balance sheet for Distributors, Inc.

Distributors, Inc.
Comparative Balance Sheet
December 31, 19_1, and December 31, 19_2

	December 31		Amount of Increase or (Decrease)	Percent of Increase or (Decrease)
	19_2	19_1		
Assets				
Cash	$15,000	$16,500	_____	_____
Accounts Receivable	22,000	18,700	_____	_____
Supplies	900	864	_____	_____
Merchandise Inventory	54,000	56,700	_____	_____
Total Assets	$91,900	$92,764	_____	_____
Liabilities				
Accounts Payable	$21,000	$20,370	_____	_____
Notes Payable	24,000	27,600	_____	_____
Total Liabilities	$45,000	$47,970		
Capital				
Common Stock	$20,000	$20,000	_____	_____
Retained Earnings	26,900	24,794	_____	_____
Total Liabilities and Capital	$91,900	$92,764	_____	_____

Learning Unit 9.2

5. Using the information contained in the Income Statement and Balance Sheet for the Westside Supply Company, compute the financial ratios.

Westside Supply Company
Income Statement
Year Ended December 31, 19_2

Revenue from Sales		$190,000
Expenses:		
Cost of Merchandise Sold	$ 70,000	
Selling Expenses	55,000	
General Expenses	35,000	
Total Expenses		$160,000
Net Income		$ 30,000

Westside Supply Company
Comparative Balance Sheet
December 31, 19_1, and December 31, 19_2

	19_2	19_1
Assets:		
Current Assets	$ 70,000	$ 60,000
Plant Assets	140,000	145,000
Total Assets	$210,000	$205,000
Liabilities:		
Current Liabilities	$ 30,000	$ 25,000
Long-Term Liabilities	40,000	50,000
Total Liabilities	$ 70,000	$ 95,000
Capital:		
Common Stock	$ 50,000	$ 50,000
Retained Earnings	90,000	80,000
Total Capital	$140,000	$130,000
Total Liabilities and Capital	$210,000	$205,000

(a) Compute the current ratio for December 31, 19_2.
(b) Compute the acid test ratio for December 31, 19_2. The current assets include an inventory of $25,000
(c) Compute the ratio of plant assets to long-term liabilities on December 31, 19_2.
(d) Compute the rate of return on total assets for 19_2.
(e) Compute the rate of return on owner's equity for 19_2.
(f) Compute the inventory turnover for 19_2. The current assets include an inventory of $25,000 for 19_2 and $20,000 for 19_1.

98

Learning Unit 9.3

6. Ed's Barber Shop received the bank statement for April. The bank
    statement shows a balance of $972.00, a service charge of $3.20, and
    a charge of $8 for a safe-deposit box rental. A deposit of $920 was
    en route to the bank the day the statement was prepared. The following
    checks had been issued but had not cleared the bank: #43, $140; #46,
    $400; #47, $39. The company's records indicate a cash balance of
    $1,324.20. Prepare a bank reconciliation statement to resolve the
    discrepancies.

Ed's Barber Shop
Bank Reconciliation Statement
April 30, 19__

Balance per bank statement		$	Balance per company records		$
Add:			Add:		
		$			$
Deduct:			Deduct:		
Adjusted balance per bank statement		$____	Adjusted balance per company records		$____

7. Mid-South Realty received its March bank statement. The bank statement
    and company records reveal the following information needed for a rec-
    onciliation. The bank service charge was $2.75. There was a $5.00
    charge for collecting a note. An error of $.18 was discovered when a
    check for $142.68 was recorded on the check stub as $142.86. A deposit
    of $520 mailed on March 15 was not shown on the statement. The follow-
    ing checks were written, but not included in the bank statement: #92,
    $82.93; #93, $51.08; #95, $119.42. The bank statement balance was
    $3,042.73. The stub on the last check written in March showed a
    balance of $3,316.87. Prepare a bank reconciliation statement.

Mid-South Realty
Bank Reconciliation Statement
March 31, 19__

Balance per bank   Balance per company
statement $ records $

   Add: Add:

                  $ $

   Deduct: Deduct:

Adjusted balance   Adjusted balance
per bank statement   per bank statement
                  $ $

Chapter 10

Learning Unit 10.1

1. Distribute the net profit of $33,900 for the partnership of Allen, Jones, and Smith. The partners plan to share equally.
2. Distribute the net profit for the partnership of (a) Adams, (b) Hall, and (c) Wright. The partners' investment is Adams, $40,000; Hall, $60,000; Wright, $40,000. Using a 2:3:2 ratio, distribute the net profit of $95,900.
3. Distribute the net profit for the partnership of (a) Drew and (b) Lee. The partners have agreed upon a return based on the amount of capital invested. Drew invested $45,000 and Lee invested $15,000. There was a profit of $40,820.
4. Distribute the net profit for the partnership of (a) Cole, (b) Sharp, and (c) Tunney. Distribute the profit of $49,063 on the basis of their investment, after paying Cole a salary of $21,000. Cole invested $20,000; Sharp $60,000; and Tunney $80,000.
5. Distribute the net profit for the partnership of (a) Feris, (b) Golden, and (c) Lewis. The partners agreed to receive 6 percent interest on their investment and divide the remainder of the profit equally. Feris invested $10,000; Golden $20,000; and Lewis $20,000. Distribute the profit of $10,500.
6. (a) Collins and (b) Moss formed a partnership and agreed that Collins would invest $26,000 and Moss $52,000. The net income for the first year was $14,040. The net income is to be divided according to the amount invested after payment of 8% interest on each partner's investment. What are each partner's interest and share of the net income?

Learning Unit 10.2

7. The board of directors of the ABC Corporation declared a dividend of $24,000. What is the dividend per share if there are 16,000 shares of common stock outstanding?
8. A corporation has 36,000 shares of common stock outstanding. What is the dividend per share if a dividend of $126,000 is declared by the board of directors?
9. A corporation has 24,000 shares of 6%, $100 par, preferred stock outstanding. What is the annual dividend per share?
10. Smith Supply, Inc. has 29,000 shares of $8 preferred stock outstanding. What are the total annual dividends on the stock?
11. The K-Tex Corporation has 40,000 shares of common stock and 10,000 shares of $8 preferred stock outstanding. What is the dividend per share for (a) preferred stock and (b) common stock in a year in which $180,000 total dividends are declared?
12. A corporation has 15,000 shares of $5 cumulative preferred stock outstanding. If no dividends are declared during the first year, how much dividend per share is due the preferred stockholders the second year?
13. A corporation had a net income of $127,500 for the previous year. The board of directors voted to retain $50,000 of the net income and pay the remainder as dividends. There are 5,000 shares of 5%, $70 par, preferred stock and 15,000 shares of common stock outstanding. What is the dividend per share (a) of preferred and (b) of common stock?

Chapter 11

Learning Unit 11.1

1. Compute the ordinary interest on a 9%, $8,500 note issued for 90 days.
2. What is the ordinary interest on an 8 1/2%, $6,500 promissory note issued for 45 days?
3. Compute the simple interest on an 8%, $28,000 promissory note issued for 60 days.
4. What is the simple interest on an 11%, $15,000 promissory note issued for 125 days?
5. Compute the exact interest on a 9%, $12,000 promissory note issued for 90 days.
6. What is the exact interest on a 10 1/2%, $17,500 promissory note issued for 60 days?
7. Determine the difference between the ordinary interest and the exact interest on a 9%, $24,000 promissory note issued for 120 days.
8. Turn-Key Realtors obtained a $7,250, 8%, 90-day loan. What is the amount of ordinary interest on the loan?
9. Joan's Fashions obtained a 120-day, 9%, $6,400 loan from a dress manufacturer. Compute the simple interest for the loan.

Learning Unit 11.2

10. The interest on a 60-day, 10% loan was $20.50. What was the amount of principal on the loan?
11. The interest on a 90-day, 8% loan was $240. What was the amount borrowed?
12. A 60-day, $10,000 loan was obtained by Sam's Repair Shop. The amount of interest on the loan was $200. What was the rate of interest?
13. The Westside Landscape Company obtained a 120-day, $14,000 loan from a commercial bank. If the interest on the loan was $420, what was the rate of interest?
14. The interest on a 7%, $8,000 loan was $56. How long was the loan outstanding?
15. A 9%, $12,304 loan was obtained by Central Railroad Supply. The interest on the loan was $46.14. How long was the loan outstanding?

Learning Unit 11.3

16. Cynthia's Day Care Center borrowed $5,600 from a commercial bank on a 12%, 60-day note. What were (a) the bank discount and (b) the net proceeds on the loan?
17. BBB Rental obtained a 9%, $8,000 loan from a commercial bank for 90 days. What were (a) the bank discount and (b) the net proceeds on the loan?
18. What is the due date on a 60-day note issued on March 4?
19. A 90-day promissory note was issued on September 17. What is the maturity date of the note?
20. Dillard's Office Machine Company accepted a 90-day note from one of its customers in payment of an open account on May 21. What is the due date of the note?
21. Northcutt Realty discounted a 60-day, $3,000 noninterest-bearing note dated March 18 at the bank on April 5. The bank discount rate is 8%. (a) What is the maturity date of the note? (b) How many days are included in the discount period? What are (c) the bank discount and (d) the net proceeds on the note?

22. Noreen's Sporting Goods received a 9%, 90-day, $2,000 note from a customer dated September 4. The note was discounted at the bank on October 21. The bank discount rate is 10%. What are (a) the maturity date, (b) the amount of interest, and (c) the maturity value of the note? What are (d) the discount period, (e) the bank discount, and (f) the net proceeds on the note?

Chapter 12

Learning Unit 12.1

1. Compute the compound interest on a one-year loan for $1,500. Interest is compounded semiannually at an annual rate of nine percent.
2. What is the amount of compound interest on a one-year loan for $2,250? Interest on the loan is compounded quarterly at an annual rate of 12 percent.
3. What is the difference between simple interest and compound interest on an investment of $2,400 at six percent for one year? Compound interest should be computed semiannually.
4. What is the maturity value of a $5,350 loan for one year with interest compounded quarterly at an annual rate of 10 percent?

Learning Unit 12.2

5. Sara Wilson would like to take a trip two years from now. What rate of interest must she earn on $5,000 in order to have $6,000 in two years if interest is compounded quarterly?
6. John Sawyer is interested in buying a local barber shop with cash. The owner is asking $7,500 for the equipment and goodwill. John has one year to raise the money. If interest is compounded semiannually and John has $7,000 now, what interest rate must he earn?
7. How long will $3,500 have to be invested at 8% compounded quarterly in order to mature to $5,000?
8. Nancy B. has $2,500 in a savings account that pays 6% compounded semi-annually. Assuming no further deposits, how long will it take for her money to earn $700 in interest?

Learning Unit 12.3

9. What is the present value of $60,000 if 10% interest is compounded quarterly for five years?
10. How much money should be invested today in order to have $100,000 in 20 years if interest of 8% is compounded quarterly?

Learning Unit 12.4

11. If $150 is deposited every three months in an account earning 6% compounded quarterly, how much will the account be worth in five years?
12. How many full payments will be received from an annuity that costs $10,000 if the payments are $500 a quarter and 8% interest is compounded quarterly?
13. How much money must be deposited today in order to withdraw $1,200 a year for the next ten years if 8 percent interest is compounded annually?
14. If $100 is deposited every month in an account earning 6% compounded monthly, what will the value of the account be in four years?

Chapter 13

Learning Unit 13.1

Using the APR tables, determine the APR for the following credit transactions.
1. Finance charge, $70; amount financed, $780; number of payments, 15.
2. Finance charge, $80; amount financed, $540; number of payments, 24.
3. Finance charge, $10; amount financed, $100; number of payments, 10.
Using the APR tables, determine the finance charges and APR for each of the following purchases.
4. Cash price, $467; down payment, $40; 20 monthly payments at $24 each.
5. Cash price, $350; down payment, 1/10; 10 monthly payments at $34 each.
6. Cash price, $550; down payment, $75; 30 monthly payments at $20 each.

Learning Unit 13.2

Determine the ending balance and APR for the following open-end accounts.
7. Beginning balance, $220; payment, $50; finance rate, 1%.
8. Beginning balance, $85; payment, $15; finance rate, 1 1/4%.
Determine the ending balance for each of the following open-end accounts.
9. Beginning balance $176.90; payment, $45; finance rate, 1 3/4%.
10. Beginning balance, $138; purchases, $34.50; payment, $30; finance rate, 1 1/2%.
11. Beginning balance, $137.70; purchases, $47.95; payment, $45; finance rate, 1 1/4%.
12. Beginning balance, $219.76; payment, $110; finance rate, 3/4%.

Chapter 14

Learning Unit 14.1

1. What is the price of a share of ACF stock that is currently quoted at 38 1/2?
2. What is the price per share for Nabisco common stock if the current quotation is 26 1/8?
3. The net income for the ABC Corporation for the past year was $325,000. The company has 50,000 shares of common stock outstanding. What were the earnings per share?
4. Northeast Manufacturing, Inc. has 26,100 shares of common stock outstanding. If the corporation's net income for the year is $84,825, what are the earnings per share?
5. The common stock of IBM is selling for $304 per share. The current earnings per share are $11.50. What are (a) the price-earnings ratio and (b) the dividend yield on the stock?
6. The XYZ Corporation had net income after taxes of $52,800. Dividends on preferred stock were $30,000. The corporation has 57,000 shares of common stock outstanding, which is currently selling for $5 per share. Total dividends of $41,400 were declared. What were the earnings per share of the common stock?

Learning Unit 14.2

7. Borden $1,000, 5 3/4% bonds are currently quoted at 80. (a) What is the price per bond? (b) What is the annual interest on the bonds?
8. Chrysler $1,000, 8% bonds are currently quoted at 75 1/4. (a) What is the price per bond? (b) What is the annual interest on the bonds?
9. Con Edison $1,000, 7 3/4% bonds are currently quoted at 85 1/2. What are (a) the current price per bond, (b) the annual interest, and (c) the yield on the bonds?
10. LTV $1,000, 5% bonds are being quoted at 56. What are (a) the price, (b) the semiannual interest, and (c) the current yield per bond?
11. Interest on MGM 10%, $1,000 bonds, which are currently quoted at 99 1/2, is paid semiannually on June 30 and December 31. What is the total cost of a bond, disregarding brokerage fees, purchased on November 30?

Chapter 15

Learning Unit 15.1

1. A real estate broker made arrangements for the sale of some commercial property for $215,000. Her rate of commission is six percent. What was the amount of commission on the sale?

2. A residence was sold for $74,500. The broker's rate of commission is seven percent. The associate handling the sale of the property received 40 percent of the broker's commission. How much commission did the associate receive?

3. The real estate broker's commission on the sale of residential property for $54,000 was $3,240. What is the broker's rate of commission?

4. A real estate broker charges 7 percent commission for handling the sale of residential property. What was the sales price of property on which the commission was $7,840?

5. Paul Verble's house was sold for $66,750. The associate involved in the sale of the property received 45 percent of the broker's six percent commission. How much commission did the associate receive?

6. A real estate broker charged $6,240 commission for handling the sale of property for $104,000. What was the rate of commission?

7. The real estate broker's commission on the sale of a lot was $495. The broker's rate of commission was 11 percent. What was the selling price of the lot?

Learning Unit 15.2

8. The sales price of a property was $79,000. The rate for title insurance is $6.25 per thousand. What is the cost of title insurance for the property?

9. ACE Service Company purchased some property for $126,000. The attorney's fee for the sale was $350 and the cost of title insurance for the property was $4.95 per thousand. What was the total of legal fees and title assurance charges?

10. An $84,000 loan on property purchased by Duvall Pontiac Company was subject to a one-point loan origination fee and two mortgage discount points. What were the loan-related charges?

11. Sherry West is obtaining a $74,600, 9% VA loan from Central Savings and Loan Association. The current market rate of interest is 9 3/4%. (a) How many mortgage discount points will be required to obtain the loan? (b) How much mortgage discount or prepaid interest will Sherry have to pay the savings and loan?

Learning Unit 15.3

12. The market value of a property is $64,000. The assessment rate for tax purposes is 65 percent, and the tax rate per hundred is $1.48. What is the annual property tax?

13. Nancy Wells owns property that has a market value of $83,000. The assessment rate is 85 percent, and the tax rate per hundred is $2.15. What is the annual property tax?

14. Property owned by Bill Shipman has a market value of $68,500. The assessment rate is 75 percent, and the tax rate per thousand is $13.35. What is the annual property tax?

15. Property that has a market value of $96,000 is subject to an assessment rate of 65 percent. What is the assessed value of the property?

Learning Unit 15.4

16. Sherman's Appliance Center pays a monthly rental of $345 plus seven percent of gross sales. Last year the gross sales were $213,000. What was the total rent for the year?

17. Miller Novelties has a lease that requires $275 per month base rent plus three percent of gross sales. If total sales for the year were $245,600, what was the average monthly rent?

18. ABC Muffler Shops paid a total rent of $6,700 last year on gross sales of $95,714.29. The lease does not include a base rental. What percentage rate is required by the lease?

19. Cowan Security Systems, Inc. pays a base rental of $185 per month plus a percentage of gross sales. If total sales for the year were $568,200 and total rent paid was $19,246, what percentage rate was contained in the lease?

Chapter 16

Learning Unit 16.1

1. Sue Brown's automobile was involved in a single car accident that
   caused $1,345 damage to her car. Her automobile policy provided $200
   deductible collision coverage at the time of the loss. How much reim-
   bursement will she receive from her insurance company for the loss?

2. Craig's automobile was involved in an accident in which two persons
   won claims for bodily injury liability limits. The first claim was
   for $7,000 and the second claim for $14,000. How much will his insurance company pay?

3. The premium for $200 deductible collision insurance on an automobile
   is $173. The premium for $50 deductible collision insurance is 157%
   of the premium for $200 deductible collision. How much more premium
   will an insured have to pay for $50 deductible collision coverage?

4. Pam Spencer has an automobile insurance policy that provides 10/20
   bodily injury limits. The premium for this coverage is $103. The
   premium for 20/40 maximum limits is 129% of the basic 10/20 rates.
   How much more premium will Pam have to pay for 20/40 bodily injury
   protection?

5. The premium for property damage liability for a maximum limit of
   $5,000 is $127. How much more premium will an insured have to pay for
   $25,000 limits if the premium is 108% of the premium for $5,000
   coverage?

Learning Unit 16.2

6. The annual premium rate per $100 coverage on a one-year, $65,000 fire
   policy is $.196. What is the premium for the policy?

7. The annual premium rate per $100 coverage on a $65,000 fire policy is
   $.182. What is the premium for the policy?

8. A $92,000 fire policy was cancelled at the request of the insured.
   The annual premium rate per $100 is $.265. The short-rate premium is
   32 percent of the annual premium. What are (a) the annual premium and
   (b) the short-rate premium for the policy?

9. The premium for a one-year fire policy issued to Rob Robbins was $245.
   The policy was returned to the insurance company for cancellation and
   is subject to a short-rate premium of 64 percent. How much return
   premium will the company forward to Rob?

10. The home of John Jenkins is covered by a $56,000 fire policy that con-
    tains an 80 percent coinsurance clause. The home is valued at $75,000.
    If the home is damaged by fire to the extent of $6,000, how much
    indemnity will John receive from the insurance company?

Learning Unit 16.3

11. What is the monthly premium for a $20,000 20-year endowment policy for
    a female, 25 years of age? The rate per $1,000 is $35.18.

12. The premium rate per $1,000 for an ordinary life policy for a female at
    age 40 is $17.18. (a) What is the annual premium for a $15,000 policy?
    (b) How much is the quarterly premium if the quarterly rate is 26 per-
    cent of the annual premium?

13. A five-year renewable-term policy for a male at age 30 is subject to a
    premium rate of $2.88 per $1,000. (a) What is the annual premium for
    a $50,000 policy? (b) The monthly rate is nine percent of the annual
    rate. How much is the monthly premium on the policy?

14. Joan Neff plans to purchase a $10,000, 20-pay life policy on her 20th
     birthday. The annual rate is $16.44 per thousand and the monthly rate
     is nine percent of the annual rate. How much annual savings will she
     realize if she elects an annual payment rather than monthly payments?

Chapter 17

Learning Unit 17.1

Find the charge for shipping the following. Round your answer to the nearest cent.
1. 3,600 pounds at $1.27 cwt.
2. 29,700 pounds at $18.25 per ton
3. 24,200 pounds at $33.60 per long ton
Using the following rate schedule, determine the charge for each of the
following shipments.

Rate Schedule Dallas to Houston	
Minimum Weight	cwt. Rate
1,000	$2.39
10,000	1.97
20,000	1.85
34,000	1.50
50,000	1.34

4. 8,100 pounds
5. 13,400 pounds
6. 7,290 pounds

Learning Unit 17.2

Determine the break point and minimum charge for the following weight
classifications.
7. Minimum weight of Class I, 2,000 pounds; cwt. rate, $1.76; minimum
    weight of Class II, 13,000 pounds; cwt. rate, $1.62
8. Minimum weight of Class II, 13,000 pounds; cwt. rate, $1.62; minimum
    weight of Class III, 25,000 pounds; cwt. rate, $1.45
9. Minimum weight of Class III, 25,000 pounds; cwt. rate, $1.45; minimum
    weight of Class IV, 40,000 pounds; cwt. rate, $1.27
Using the following rate schedule, determine the transportation cost for
each of the following shipments.

Rate Schedule

Memphis to Nashville				Memphis to Knoxville			
Minimum Weight	T Rate	Minimum Charge	Break Point	Minimum Weight	T Rate	Minimum Charge	Break Point
10,000	$23.00	$115	25,806	10,000	$26.00	$130	42,307
40,000	20.00	400	56,000	50,000	22.00	550	69,090
70,000	16.00	560	87,500	80,000	19.00	760	101,052
100,000	14.00	700	117,857	120,000	16.00	960	121,875
150,000	11.00	825		150,000	13.00	975	

STOP-OFF CHARGE: $50.00

10. Would it be less expensive to pay separate shipping charges or combined shipping charges on the following two shipments? What is the difference between the two alternatives? 90,000 pounds to Nashville, 90,000 pounds to Knoxville.

11. Would it be less expensive to pay separate shipping charges or combined shipping charges on the following two shipments? What is the difference between the two alternatives? 60,000 pounds to Nashville, 75,000 pounds to Knoxville.

Chapter 18

Learning Unit 18.1

1. What is the (a) mean, (b) median, and (c) mode for the following ungrouped
   data? 17   25   27   39   17   15   28
2. On his last trip, a traveling salesman purchased gasoline nine times.
   The amounts charged to his credit card were: $19.90, $21.50, $16.95,
   $10.00, $18.75, $19.90, $17.60, $20.15, and $12.50. What were the
   (a) mean, (b) median, and (c) mode for this list of gasoline charges?

Learning Unit 18.2

3. Set up a frequency distribution with the following raw data and class
   intervals: data--62, 64, 51, 73, 68, 51, 57, 69, 73, 74, 58, 56, 52,
   67, 54, 59, 66, 69, 51, 57, 63, 66, 50, 74, 68; class intervals--
   50-54, 55-59, 60-64, 65-69, and 70-74.
   (a) What is the mean?
   (b) What is the median?
   (c) What is the modal class?
4. Construct a frequency distribution and find the (a) median, (b) mean,
   and (c) modal class. The raw data and class intervals are: employee
   monthly income--$850; $900; $1,050; $1,200; $975; $1,000; $1,500;
   $1,380; $960; $1,080; $1,080; $1,450; $875; $995; $1,010; $1,360;
   $1,250; $1,180; $1,125; $1,025; $1,070; $1,225; $1,100; $1,080; $1,100;
   $1,200; class intervals--850-949; 950-1,049; 1,050-1,149; 1,150-1,249;
   1,250-1,349; 1,350-1,449; 1,450-1,549.

Learning Unit 18.3

5. Construct a vertical bar graph showing sales for the years 1975-1980:
   $2,075,000; $2,000,200; $3,010,000; $4,500,000; $4,300,000; $5,000,100.
6. Ace Office Supply recorded sales of $600,000 last year. Ace's three
   salesmen--Jerry, Ron, and Bob--had respective sales of $100,000;
   $200,000; $300,000. Draw a circle graph showing each salesman's percent of total sales.
7. Sandra's records indicate that the cost of paper for her print shop
   has been increasing over the past five years beginning with 1975. Use
   a line graph to show her cost per ream for each year: $3.90, $4.20,
   $5.10, $5.93, $6.15.

Test Bank Answer Key

Chapter 1

1.   two hundred sixty-four
2.   one thousand eight hundred ninety-eight
3.   28,000   4. 3,803
5.   thousand   6. ten thousand
7.   2   8.   4
9.   ninety-three hundredths
10. one hundred fifty-seven thousandths
11. .76   12.   .51   13.   .01
14. $186.52   15. $720
16. 1,864   17. 2,253
18. 2,083 + 1,732 + 2,147 = 5,962
19. 2,110 + 1,710 + 812 = 4,632
20. 407   21. 919   22. 2,142   23. 5,813
24. 598,851   25. 10,329,198
26. 77 R18   27. 45 R32
28. 21 x $36 = $756   29. 2,604/6 = 434
30. $315 x 4 = $1,260   31. $624/$4 = 156
32. 291.352   33. 1,661.861   34. $132.88   35.   41.84
36. $176.24 + $324.09 + $287.55 + $87.96 = $875.84
37. $27.98 - $20.47 = $7.51
38. $.60 + $1.19 + $.38 + $.47 = $2.64
     $10.00 - $2.64 = $7.36
39. $2.72   40. 2.83122 (2.83)   41. 14.90   42. 29.418
43. 840   44. 8.2   45. 3,420   46. .9
47. $36.96/$.28 = 132
48. 1,323/14.7 = 90
49. $15.86 x 14.75 = $233.94

Chapter 2

1. 5/9   2. 1/3   3. 54   4. 8
5. 4 5/7   6. 5 3/11   7. 29/6   8. 77/9
9. .375   10. .2857   11. 19/100   12. 3/5
13. 27/36 + 16/36 + 15/36 = 58/36 = 1 11/18
14. 14 50/70 + 3 35/70 + 22 14/70 = 40 29/70
15. 38/42 - 35/42 = 3/42 = 1/14
16. 35/45 - 6/45 = 29/45
17. 1/5 + 1/12 = 12/60 + 5/60 = 17/60
18. 4/9 + 1/4 = 16/36 + 9/36 = 25/36
     36/36 - 25/36 = 11/36
19. 1 3/16 + 27 14/16 = 28 17/16 = 29 1/16
20. 6/35   21. 11/27   22. 3/16   23. 3/22
24. 89/3 = 29 2/3   25. 60 3/10   26. 15/14 = 1 1/14
27. 32   28. 55/118   29. 49/66
30. 900 x 1/5 = 180
31. 45 ÷ 3/7 = 45 x 7/3 = 105
32. 48 ÷ 4 = 12
     12 x 1 3/4 = 12 x 7/4 = 21

Chapter 3

1. .3761   2. .0075   3. 263%   4. 3.5%
5. 3/4   6. 39/100   7. 12.5%   8. 66.67%
9. 18   10. 11   11. 12   12. 5
13. 3   14. 2 1/3   15. 21   16. 5
17. $375 x .12 = $45
18. $6.45 x .072 = $.46
19. $2.67/.035 = $76.29
20. 125.21/.08375 = 1,495.04
21. $60/$750 = .08 = 8%
22. $95/$865 = 11%
23. $865 x .15 = $129.75
24. $82.96 x .06 = $4.98
25. $1,700 x .80 = $1,360
26. $470 - $329 = $141
     $141/$470 = 30%
27. 22,600/27,400 = 82%
28. $2,550/$42,500 = .06 = 6%
29. $51.05/.065 = $785.38
30. $101.64/.11 = $924

Chapter 4

1. $120 x .70 = $84
2. $720 x .82 = $590.40
3. 1.00 - .30 = .70
    1.00 - .20 = .80
    1.00 - .10 = .90
    .70 x .80 x .90 = .504 = 50.4%
    100% - 50.4% = 49.6%
4. 1.00 - .25 = .75
    1.00 - .15 = .85
    1.00 - .10 = .90
    .75 x .85 x .90 = .57375 = 57.375%
    100% - 57.375% = 42.625%

5. 1.00 - .20 = .80
    1.00 - .10 = .90
    .80 x .90 = .72
    $118.70 x .72 = $85.46
6. 1.00 - .25 = .75
    1.00 - .15 = .85
    .75 x .85 = .6375
    $87.40 x .6375 = $55.72
7. 1.00 - .20 = .80
    1.00 - .10 = .90
    .80 x .90 = .72
    $196.35 x .72 = $141.37
8. (a) 1.00 - .40 = .60
        1.00 - .10 = .90
        .60 x .90 = .54
        $7,700 x .54 = $4,158
        1.00 - .30 = .70
        1.00 - .20 = .80
        .70 x .80 = .56
        $7,500 x .56 = $4,200
        Bid A ($4,158) is less than Bid B ($4,200)
    (b) $4,200 - $4,158 = $42
9. (a) 1.00 - .15 = .85
        1.00 - .10 = .90
        .85 x .90 = .765
        $2,360 x .765 = $1,805.40 Trade Price
    (b) $1,805.40 + $47.60 = $1,853 Billing Price
10. $187.65 x .02 = $3.75
    $187.65 - $3.75 = $183.90
11. $417.65 x .03 = $12.53
    $417.65 - $12.53 = $405.12
12. June 8, August 17
13. December 21, February 4
14. $176.40 - $36.40 = $140.00
    $140.00 x .02 = $2.80
    $140.00 - $2.80 = $137.20
    $137.20 + $11.40 = $148.60
15. $136.47 - $35.00 = $101.47
    $101.47 x .03 = $3.04
    $101.47 - $3.04 = $98.43
    $98.43 + $5.00 = $103.43
16. $128.67 x .02 = $2.57
    $128.67 - $2.57 = $126.10
17. $362.50 - $17.40 = $345.10
    $345.10 x .02 = $6.90
    $345.10 - $6.90 = $338.20
18. $245/.98 = $250
    $748.50 - $250 = $498.50
19. $606.25/.97 = $625.00
    $1,260.73 - $625.00 = $635.73
20. 1.00 - .15 = .85
    1.00 - .10 = .90
    .85 x .9 = .765
    $900 x .765 = $688.50
    $688.50 x .98 = $674.73
21. $426.82 - $49.66 = $377.16
    $377.16 x .98 = $369.62
    $369.62 + $12.40 = $382.02
22. $320.00/.96 = $333.33
    $750.00 - $333.33 = $416.67

Chapter 5

1. $78 + $51 = $129
2. $22.40 x 1.48 = $33.15
3. $22.70 x 1.38 = $31.33
4. $14.74/1.53 = $9.63
5. $51.00/1.20 = $42.50
6. $9.53 - $7.60 = $1.93
    1.93/7.60 = .25 = 25%
7. $19.98 - $13.50 = $6.48
    6.48/13.50 = .48 = 48%
8. $6.92/.54 = $12.81
9. $20.90/.52 = $40.19
10. $5.50 - $4.30 = $1.20
    $1.20/$5.50 = .22 = 22%
11. $19.98 - $13.50 = $6.48
    $6.48/$19.98 = .32 = 32%
12. $90.00/.75 = $120.00
13. $24.95 - $18.75 = $6.20
    $6.20/$24.95 = .25 = 25%
14. $146.60/1.40 = $104.71
15. 200 x $.25 = $50
    .30 x $50 = $15
    $50 + $15 = $65
    200 x .20 = 40
    200 - 40 = 160
    $65/160 = $.41
16. $25 + $45 = $70
    $70 x .40 = $28
    $70 + $28 = $98
    500 x .20 = 100
    500 - 100 = 400
    $98/400 = $.25
17. $99.95 - $15.60 = $84.35
18. $75.00 - $40.00 = $35.00
    $35/$75 = .47 = 47%
19. $50.15 - $38.58 = $11.57
    $11.57/$50.15 = .23 = 23%
20. $40.35 - $26.90 = $13.45
    $13.45/$26.90 = .50 = 50%
21. $52.70 - $37.64 = $15.06
    $15.06/$37.64 = .40 = 40%
22. $31.50 x .86 = $27.09
23. $12.99 x .75 = $9.74
24. $87/1.4 = $62.14
25. $14.25/1.3 = $10.96
26. $194.95 x $.77 = $150.11
27. $2.97 - $1.88 = $1.09
    $1.09/$1.88 = .58 = 58%

Chapter 6

1. $288 x 52 = $14,976
    $14,976/12 = $1,248
2. $11,688/24 = $487
3. $1,040 x 12 = $12,480
    $12,480/52 = $240

4. $7.75 x 40 = $310.00
    $11.625 x 6 = $69.75
    $310.00 + $69.75 = $379.75
5. $9.45 x 40 = $378.00
    $14.175 x 3 = $42.53
    $378.00 + $42.53 = $420.53
6. $2.80 x 42 = $117.60
    43 x $4.00 = $172.00
    $117.60 + $172.00 = $289.60
7. $2.80 x 45.5 = $127.40
    39 x $4.00 = $156.00
    $127.40 + $156.00 = $283.40
8. $4,000 x .05 = $200.00
    $1,700 x .07 = $119.00
    $200.00 + $119.00 = $319.00
9. $5,000 x .03 = $150.00
    $3,250 x .05 = $162.50
    $100.00 + $150.00 + $162.50 = $412.50
10. (a) $1,600 x .0613 = $98.08
    (b) $197.60
    (c) $1,600 - $295.68 = $1,304.32
11. (40 x $4.80) + (7.5 x $7.20) = $246
    $246 - (4 x $19.23) = $169.08
    $12.15 + (.18 x 42.08) = $19.62
    $246 x .0613 = $15.08
    $246 - ($19.62 + $15.08 + $10.00) = $201.30

Chapter 7

1. $9,800 - $1,000 = $8,800
    $8,800/4 = $2,200
2. $25,000 - $5,000 = $20,000
    $20,000/10 = $2,000
3. $13,000 + $325 + $37 = $13,362
4. (a) $9,600 - $3,600 = $6,000
        $6,000/3 = $2,000
    (b) $9,600 - $2,000 = $7,600
5. $9,800 - $1,000 = $8,800
    $8,800/100,000 = $.088
    $.088 x 28,000 = $2,464
6. $135,000 - $9,000 = $126,000
    $126,000/20,000 = $6.30
    $6.30 x 2,230 = $14,049.00
7. (a) 6(6 + 1)/2 = 42/2 = 21
        6/21 = 2/7
    (b) 4/21
8. (a) 8(8 + 1)/2 = 72/2 = 36
        $14,016 - $2,400 = $11,616.00
        $11,616 x 8/36 = $2,581.33
    (b) $14,016 - $2,581.33 = $11,434.67
9. 7(7 + 1)/2 = 56/2 = 28
    $42,200 - $7,000 = $35,200
    7/28 x $35,200 = $8,800
    1/3 x $8,800 = $2,933.33
10. 100%/8 = 1.00/8 = .125 = 12.5%
    12.5% x 2 = 25%

118

11. (a) $14,016 x .25 = $3,504
     (b) $14,016 - $3,504 = $10,512
12. 100%/7 = 14.2857%
     14.2857% x 2 = 28.57%
     $42,200 x .2857 = $12,056.54
     $12,056.54 x 1/3 = $4,018.85

Chapter 8

1. (a) 3 x $36 = $108
         2 x $39 = $ 78
         4 x $40 = $160
                   $346

    (b) 7 x $40 = $280
         2 x $39 = $ 78
                   $358

    (c) 6 x $34 = $204
         3 x $36 = $108
                   $312

    (d)   6 x $34 = $ 204
         10 x $36 = $ 360
         15 x $37 = $ 555
          8 x $39 = $ 312
          7 x $40 = $ 280
         46          $1,711

         $1,711/46 = $37.196 average cost per unit
         $37.196 x 9 = $334.76

2. (a) 1 x $126 = $126
         1 x $130 = $130
         4 x $125 = $500
                    $756

    (b) 6 x $125 = $750

    (c) 2 x $115 = $230
         4 x $126 = $504
                    $734

    (d)   2 x $115 = $ 230
         30 x $126 = $ 3,780
         20 x $128 = $ 2,560
         20 x $130 = $ 2,600
         10 x $125 = $ 1,250
         82           $10,420

         $10,420/82 = $127.073 average cost per unit
         $127.073 x 6 = $762.44

3. $ 45,000
                    $324,000
                    + 15,000
                    $339,000
          $12,000
            6,200   18,200   320,800
                                $365,800
                                - 47,000
                                $318,800

4. $ 32,000
                    $290,000
                    + 13,000
                    $303,000
          $ 9,000
          + 5,600   - 14,600   +288,400
                                $320,400
                                - 30,000
                                $290,400

Chapter 9

1. 50.00, 9.00, 16.00, 3.00, 2.00, 80.00, 20.00
2. 7.00, 25.00, 1.00, 45.00, 22.00, 23.00, 25.00, 48.00, 52.00
3. $19,700, 11.11%
    $13,700, 11.11%
    $720, 4.17%
    $511, 7.53%
    $140, 16.28%
    $15,071, 10.17%
    $4,629, 15.92%
4. ($1,500), (9.09%)
    $3,300, 17.65%
    $36, 4.17%
    ($2,700), (4.76%)
    ($864), (.93%)
    $630, 3.09%
    ($3,600), 13.04%
    ($2,970), (6.19%)
    0, 0
    $2,106, 8.49%
    ($864), (.93%)
5. (a) 2.33:1
    (b) 1.5:1
    (c) 3.5:1
    (d) 14.29%
    (e) 21.43%
    (f) 3.11 times
6. $1,313.00
7. $3,309.30

Chapter 10

1. $11,300
2. (a) $95,900/7 = $13,700
        $13,700 x 2 = $27,400

(b) $13,700 x 3 = $41,100
(c) $13,700 x 2 = $27,400

3. (a) $45,000 + $15,000 = $60,000
        ($45,000/$60,000) x $40,820 = $30,615
    (b) ($15,000/$60,000) x $40,820 = $10,205

4. $49,063 - $21,000 = $28,063
    $20,000 + $60,000 + $80,000 = $160,000
    (a) $28,063 x $20,000/$160,000 = $3,507.88 + $21,000 = $24,507.88
    (b) $28,063 x $60,000/$160,000 = $10,523.63
    (c) $28,063 x $80,000/$160,000 = $14,031.50

5. .06 x $10,000 = $ 600 Feris
    .06 x $20,000 = $1,200 Golden
    .06 x $20,000 = $1,200 Lewis
                    $3,000 Total interest

    $10,500 - $3,000 = $7,500
    $7,500/3 = $2,500
    (a) $600 + $2,500 = $3,100
    (b) $1,200 + $2,500 = $3,700
    (c) $1,200 + $2,500 = $3,700

6. .08 x $26,000 = $2,080 Collins
    .08 x $52,000 = $4,160 Moss
                    $6,240 Total interest

    $14,040 - $6,240 = $7,800
    $26,000 + $52,000 = $78,000
    (a) ($26,000/$78,000) x $7,800 = $2,600 Collins
    (b) ($52,000/$78,000) x $7,800 = $5,200 Moss

7. $24,000/16,000 = $1.50

8. $126,000/36,000 = $3.50

9. $100 x .06 = $6

10. 29,000 x $8 = $232,000

11. (a) $8 per share preferred
        10,000 x $8 = $80,000 total preferred
    (b) $180,000 - $80,000 = $100,000 total common
        $100,000/40,000 = $2.50 per share common

12. $5 (first year) + $5 (second year) = $10 dividend due preferred

13. (a) .05 x $70 = $3.50 per share preferred
        $3.50 x $5,000 = $17,500 total preferred
    (b) $127,500 - $50,000 = $77,500
        $77,500 - $17,500 = $60,000 total common
        $60,000/15,000 = $4 per share common

Chapter 11

1. $8,500 x .09 x 90/360 = $191.25
2. $6,500 x .085 x 45/360 = $69.06
3. $28,000 x .08 x 60/360 = $373.33
4. $15,000 x .11 x 125/360 = $572.92
5. $12,000 x .09 x 90/365 = $266.30
6. $17,500 x .105 x 60/365 = $302.05
7. $24,000 x .09 x 120/360 = $720.00
    $24,000 x .09 x 120/365 = $710.14
    $720.00 - $710.14 = $9.86
8. $7,250 x .08 x 90/360 = $145
9. $6,400 x .09 x 120/360 = $192

10. $20.50/(.1 \times 60/360) = \$1,230$

11. $240/(.08 \times 90/360) = \$12,000$

12. $200/(\$10,000 \times 60/360) = .12 = 12\%$

13. $420/(\$14,000 \times 120/360) = 420/4,666.67 = .08999 = 9\%$

14. $56/(\$8,000 \times .07) = 56/560 = .1$
    $.1 \times 360 = 36$ days

15. $46.14/(\$12,304 \times .09) = \$46.14/1,107.36 = .0416667$
    $.0416667 \times 360 = 15$ days

16. (a) $5,600 \times .12 \times 60/360 = \$112$
    (b) $5,600 - \$112 = \$5,488$

17. (a) $8,000 \times .09 \times 90/360 = \$180$
    (b) $8,000 - \$180 = \$7,820$

18. $31 - 4 = $ 27 days in March
    $60 - 27 = $ 33 days remaining
              -30 days in April
                3 days in May

19. $30 - 17 = $ 13 days in September
    $90 - 13 = $ 77 days remaining
              -31 days in October
                46 days remaining
              -30 days in November
                16 days in December

20. $31 - 21 = $ 10 days in May
    $90 - 10 = $ 80 days remaining
              -30 days in June
                50 days remaining
              -31 days in July
                19 days in August

21. (a) $31 - 18 = $ 13 days in March
        $60 - 13 = $ 47 days remaining
                  -30 days in April
                    17 days in May

    (b) $30 - 5 = $ 25 days in April
                $+17$ days in May
                  42 days

    (c) $3,000 \times .08 \times 42/360 = \$28$
    (d) $3,000 - \$28 = \$2,972$

22. (a) $30 - 4 = $ 26 days in September
        $90 - 26 = $ 64 days remaining
                  -31 days in October
                    33 days remaining
                  -30 days in November
                    3 days in December

    (b) $2,000 \times .09 \times 90/360 = \$45$
    (c) $2,000 + \$45 = \$2,045$
    (d) $31 - 21 = $ 10 days in October
                  $+30$ days in November
                  $+ 3$ days in December
                    43 days

    (e) $2,045 \times .1 \times 43/360 = \$24.43$
    (f) $2,045 - \$24.43 = \$2,020.57$

Chapter 12

1. $1,500 x .09 x 1/2 = $67.50
   $1,500 + $67.50 = $1,567.50
   $1,567.50 x .09 x 1/2 = $70.54
   $67.50 + $70.54 = $138.04
2. $2,250 x .12 x 1/4 = $67.50
   $2,250 + $67.50 = $2,317.50
   $2,317.50 x .12 x 1/4 = $69.53
   $2,317.50 + $69.53 = $2,387.03
   $2,387.03 x .12 x 1/4 = $71.61
   $2,387.03 + $71.61 = $2,458.64
   $2,458.64 x .12 x 1/4 = $73.76
   $67.50 + $69.53 + $71.61 + $73.76 = $282.40
3. $2,400 x .06 x 1 = $144 simple interest
   $2,400 x .06 x 1/2 = $72
   $2,400 + $72 = $2,472
   $2,472 x .06 x 1/2 = $74.16
   $72 + $74.16 = $146.16 compound interest
   $146.16 - $144 = $2.16
4. $5,350 x .1 x 1/4 = $133.75
   $5,350 + $133.75 = $5,483.75
   $5,483.75 x .1 x 1/4 = $137.09
   $5,483.75 + $137.09 = $5,620.84
   $5,620.84 x .1 x 1/4 = $140.52
   $5,620.84 + $140.52 = $5,761.36
   $5,761.36 x .1 x 1/4 = $144.03
   $133.75 + $137.09 + $140.52 + $144.03 = $555.39

5. $MV/P = (1 + i)^n$; $n = 8$

   $$\$6,000/\$5,000 = (1 + i)^8; \quad 1.2 = (1 + i)^4$$
   i = 2 1/2% from compound interest table
   R = 10% (2 1/2% x 4)

6. $MV/P = (1 + i)^n$; $n = 2$

   $$\$7,500/\$7,000 = (1 + i)^2; \quad 1.07142857 = (1 + i)^2$$
   i = 4% from compound interest table
   R = 8% (4% x 2)

7. $MV/P = (1 + i)^n$; $i = 8\%/4 = 2\%$

   $$\$5,000/\$3,500 = (1 + 2\%)^n; \quad 1.42857142 = (1 + 2\%)^n$$
   n = 19 from compound interest table
   Time = 4 years, 9 months

8. MV = $2,500 + $700 or $3,200; i = 6%/2 = 3%

   $$MV/P = (1 + i)^n; \quad \$3,200/\$2,500 = (1 + 3\%)^n$$

   $$1.28 = (1 + 3\%)^n$$
   n = 9 from compound interest table
   Time = 4 years, 6 months

9. $PV = MV \times 1/(1 + i)^n$; $i = 10\%/4 = 2\ 1/2\%$; $n = 20$
   PV = $60,000 x .61027094 (from PV table)
   PV = $36,616.26

10. $PV = MV \times 1/(1 + i)^n$; $i = 8\%/4 = 2\%$; $n = 80$
    PV = $100,000 x .20510973 (from PV table)
    PV = $20,510.97

11. $MV = P \cdot Sn\rceil i$; $i = 1\ 1/2\%$; $n = 20$
    $MV = \$150 \times 25.54465761$ (from MV of an Annuity table)
    $MV = \$3,831.70$

12. $PV = P \cdot An\rceil i$; $i = 8\%/4 = 2\%$; $n = ?$

    $PV/P = An\rceil i$; $\$10,000/\$500 = An\rceil 2\%$

    $20 = An\rceil 2\%$
    $n = 25$ payments (from PV of an Annuity table)

13. $PV = P \cdot An\rceil i$; $i = 8\%$; $n = 10$
    $PV = \$1,200 \times 6.71008140$ (from PV of an Annuity table)
    $PV = \$8,052.10$

14. $MV = P \cdot Sn\rceil i$; $i = 6\%/12 = 1/2\%$; $n = 48$
    $MV = \$100 \times 54.09783222$
    $MV = \$5,409.78$

Chapter 13

1. $\$70/\$780 = .08974 \times 100 = 8.974$ for 15 mos. $= 13.25\%$
2. $\$80/\$540 = .14814 \times 100 = 14.814$ for 24 mos. $= 13.75\%$
3. $\$10/\$100 = .10000 \times 100 = 10.000$ for 10 mos. $= 21.25\%$
4. $\$24 \times 20 + \$40 = \$520 - \$467 = \$53$
   $\$53/(\$470 - \$40) = .12326 \times 100 = 12.326$ for 20 mos. $= 13.5\%$
5. $\$34 \times 10 + \$35 = \$375 - \$350 = \$25$
   $\$25/(\$350 - \$35) = .07936 \times 100 = 7.936$ for 10 mos. $= 17.00\%$
6. $\$20 \times 30 + \$75 = \$675 - \$550 = \$125$
   $\$125/(\$550 - \$75) = .26316 \times 100 = 26.316$ for 30 mos. $= 19\%$
7. $\$220 \times .01 = \$2.20$
   $\$220 + \$2.20 - \$50 = \$172.20$
   $1\% \times 12 = 12\%$
8. $\$85 \times .0125 = \$1.06$
   $\$85 + \$1.06 - \$15 = \$71.06$
   $1\ 1/4\% \times 12 = 15\%$
9. $\$176.90 \times .0175 = \$3.10$
   $\$176.90 + \$3.10 - \$45 = \$135$
   $1\ 3/4\% \times 12 = 21\%$
10. $\$138 \times .015 = \$2.07$
    $\$138 + \$2.07 - \$30 + \$34.50 = \$144.57$
11. $\$137.70 \times .0125 = \$1.72$
    $\$137.70 + \$1.72 - \$45 + \$47.95 = \$142.37$
12. $\$219.76 \times .0075 = \$1.65$
    $\$219.76 + \$1.65 - \$110 = \$111.41$

Chapter 14

1. $\$38.50$
2. $\$26.125$
3. $\$325,000/50,000 = \$6.50$
4. $\$84,825/26,100 = \$3.25$
5. (a) $\$304/\$11.50 = 26.4:1$
   (b) $\$11.50/\$304 = .0378 = 3.8\%$
6. $\$52,800 - \$30,000 = \$22,800$
   $\$22,800/57,000 = \$.40$
7. (a) $.8 \times \$1,000 = \$800$
   (b) $\$1,000 \times .0575 \times 1 = \$57.50$

8. (a) .7525 x $1,000 = $752.50
    (b) $1,000 x .08 x 1 = $80
9. (a) .855 x $1,000 = $855
    (b) $1,000 x .0775 = $77.50
    (c) $77.50/$855 = .09064 = 9%
10. (a) $1,000 x .56 = $560
    (b) $1,000 x .05 x 1/2 = $25.00
    (c) $50/$560 = .089 = 8.9%
11. $1,000 x .1 x 5/12 = $41.6666 = $41.67
    $1,000 x .995 = $995
    $995 + $41.67 = $1,036.67

Chapter 15

1. $215,000 x .06 = $12,900
2. $74,500 x .07 = $5,215
    $5,215 x .40 = $2,086
3. $3,240/$54,000 = .06 = 6%
4. $7,840/.07 = $112,000
5. $66,750 x .06 = $4,005
    $4,005 x .45 = $1,802.25
6. $6,240/$104,000 = .06 = 6%
7. $495/.11 = $4,500
8. 79 x $6.25 = $493.75
9. $4.95 x 126 = $623.70
    $623.70 + $350 = $973.70
10. $84,000 x .03 = $2,520
11. (a) 6
    (b) $74,600 x .06 = $4,476
12. $64,000 x .65 = $41,600
    $1.48 x 416 = $615.68
13. $83,000 x .85 = $70,550
    $2.15 x 705.5 = $1,516.825 = $1,516.83
14. $68,500 x .75 = $51,375
    51.375 x $13.35 = $685.856 = $685.86
15. $96,000 x .65 = $62,400
16. $213,000 x .07 = $14,910
    $345 x 12 = $4,140
    $14,910 + $4,140 = $19,050
17. $245,600 x .03 = $7,368
    $275 x 12 = $3,300
    $7,368 + $3,300 = $10,668
    $10,668/12 = $889
18. $6,700/$95,714.29 = .07 = 7%
19. $185 x 12 = $2,220
    $19,246 - $2,220 = $17,026
    $17,026/$568,300 = .029975 = .03 = 3%

Chapter 16

1. $1,345 - $200 = $1,145
2. $7,000 + $10,000 = $17,000
3. $173 x 1.57 = $271.61
    $271.61 - $173 = $98.61
4. $103 x 1.29 = $132.87
    $132.87 - $103 = $29.87

5. $127 x 1.08 = $137.16
    $137.16 - $127 = $10.16
6. 650 x $.196 = $127.40
7. 650 x $.182 = $118.30
8. (a) 920 x $.265 = $243.80
    (b) $243.80 x .32 = $78.016 = $78.02
9. $245 x .64 = $156.80
10. $56,000/($75,000 x .80) x $6,000 = $5,600
11. 20 x $35.18 = $703.60
12. (a) 15 x $17.18 = $257.70
    (b) $257.70 x .26 = $67.00
13. (a) 50 x $2.88 = $144
    (b) $144 x .09 = $12.96
14. 10 x $16.44 = $164.40
    $164.40 x .09 = $14.80
    12 x $14.80 = $177.60
    $177.60 - $164.40 = $13.20

Chapter 17

1. 3,600/100 x $1.27 = $45.72
2. 29,700/2,000 x $18.25 = $271.01
3. 24,200/2,240 x $33.60 = $363.00
4. 8,100/100 x $2.39 = $193.59
5. 13,400/100 x $1.97 = $263.98
6. 7,290/100 x $2.39 = $174.23

7. $$\frac{13,000 \times (\$1.62/100)}{\$1.76/100} = 11,965$$

8. $$\frac{25,000 \times (\$1.45/100)}{\$1.62/100} = 22,376$$

9. $$\frac{40,000 \times (\$1.27/100)}{\$1.45/100} = 35,034$$

10. Separate   90,000/2,000 x $14 = $ 630
                 90,000/2,000 x $19 = ___855
                                      $1,485

    Combined   (90,000 + 90,000)/2,000 x $13 + $50 = $1,220
    Difference $1,485 - $1,220 = $265

11. Separate   60,000/2,000 x $16 = $ 480.00
                 75,000/2,000 x $19 = ___712.50
                                      $1,192.50

    Combined   (60,000 + 75,000)/2,000 x $13 + $50 = $927.50
    Difference $1,192.50 - $927.50 = $265.00

Chapter 18

1. (a) 176/7 = 25.14
    (b) 25; (15   17   17   25   27   28   29)

        $$\frac{n + 1}{2} = \frac{7 + 1}{2} = \frac{8}{2} = \text{4th position}$$

    (c) 17

2. (a) $156.10/9 = $17.34
    (b) $18.75;
        (10.00, 12.50, 16.95, 17.60, <u>18.75</u>, 19.90, 19.90, 20.15, 21.50)
        $$\frac{n + 1}{2} = \frac{9 + 1}{2} = \frac{10}{2} = \text{5th position}$$
    (c) $19.90

3. (a) 1,540/25 = 61.6
    (b) 60 + (12.5 - 11)/3 x 5 = 62.5
    (c) 65 - 69

4. (a) $1,050 + (13 - 9)/8 x 100 = $1,100
    (b) 29,400/26 = $1,130.77
    (c) $1,050 - $1,149

5.

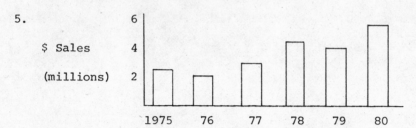

6. Jerry = 100,000/600,000 = 16 2/3%
    Ron   = 200,000/600,000 = 33 1/3%
    Bob   = 300,000/600,000 = 50%

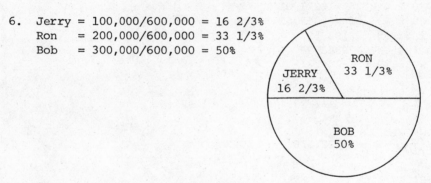

7.

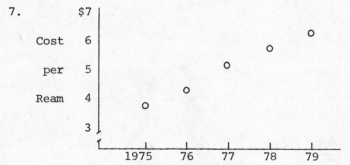

Positional Notation: Whole Numbers

Group Name	Positional Value	Positional Notation
Billions	hundred billions	100,000,000,000
	ten billions	10,000,000,000
	billions	1,000,000,000
Millions	hundred millions	100,000,000
	ten millions	10,000,000
	millions	1,000,000
Thousands	hundred thousands	100,000
	ten thousands	10,000
	thousands	1,000
Units	hundreds	100
	tens	10
	ones	1

Positional Notation: Whole Numbers and Decimal Numbers

millions	hundred thousands	ten thousands	thousands	hundreds	tens	ones	Decimal Point	tenths	hundredths	thousandths	ten-thousandths	hundred-thousandths	millionths
3	8	6	2	5	7	0	.	7	5	2	6	8	3

Whole Number   Decimal Number

← (increasing size)   (decreasing size) →

Invoice

No.

Sold To Cumbie and Cumbie
- 419 East First
- City

Shipped to Cumbie and Cumbie
- 419 East First
- City

Your Order No. 19821	Our Order No. 43061	Salesman pje		Date 4/8/19–
Date Shipped 4/8	Shipped VIA Ace Trucking	F.O.B. dest.	Terms n/30	

Quantity Ordered	Quantity Shipped	Stock Number/Description	Unit Price	Unit	Amount	
6	6	Battery Operated Grafic Clock	28 96	ea	173	76
4	4	Photo Scenic Clock	10 43	ea	41	72
10	10	L. E. D. Digital Clock	14 74	ea	147	40
20	20	Travel Alarm Clock	5 23	ea	104	60
		Total			467	48

Wilson Jones Company
GRAYLINE FORM 44-442 4 PART
© 1977 • PRINTED IN U.S.A.

Percentage Formulas

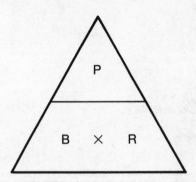

Use the delta to remember the formulas in a percentage problem.

Finding the Portion. Cover the *P*. The remaining factors are the formula for determining the portion.

$$P = B \times R$$

Finding the Base. Cover the *B*. The remaining factors are the formula for determining the base.

$$B = \frac{P}{R}$$

Finding the Rate. Cover the *R*. The remaining factors are the formula for determining the rate.

$$R = \frac{P}{B}$$

Finding the Portion

What is 16% of 800?

"Of," as used above, usually indicates that the unknown factor is the portion. Multiplication is used in solving for P.

$$P = B \times R$$
$$= 800 \times .16$$
$$= 128$$

Finding the Base

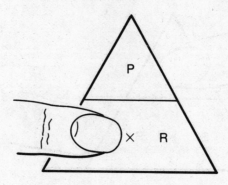

30 is 20% of what number?

"Of what," as used above, usually indicates that the unknown factor is the base. The base is also the unknown factor when the two factors given are equated, as in the statement "30 *is* 20%." Division is used in solving for *B*.

$$B = P \div R$$
$$= 30 \div .20$$
$$= 150$$

Finding the Rate

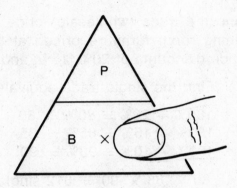

102 is what percent of 340?

"What percent," or "what rate," as used above, indicates that the unknown factor is the rate. Division is used in solving for R.

$$R = P \div B$$
$$= 102 \div 340$$
$$= .30 = 30\%$$

Trade Pricing

PROBLEM Find the trade (wholesale) price of a set of dining room furniture priced at $1,500 with trade discounts of 20%, 15%, and 10%.

Solution (1) Find the single trade equivalent.

100% − 20% = 80% = .80
100% − 15% = 85% = .85
100% − 10% = 90% = .90

.80 × .85 × .90 = .612 single trade equivalent

(2) Determine the trade price by multiplying the list price by the single trade equivalent.

$1,500 × .612 = $918 trade price

PROBLEM Find the single discount equivalent for a trade discount of 20%, 15%, and 10%.

Solution $\textit{Single discount equivalent} = 100\% - \textit{Single trade equivalent}$

$= 1.000 - .612$
$= .388 = 38.8\%$

Cash Discount

PROBLEM Find the cash discount and net amount of a $326.50 invoice with discount terms 2/10, n/30.

Solution (a) *Cash discount = Invoice amount × Rate of discount*
$$= \$326.50 \times .02$$
$$= \$6.53$$

(b) *Net amount = Invoice amount − Cash discount*
$$= \$326.50 - \$6.53$$
$$= \$319.97$$

Alternate:

Net Amount = Invoice Amount × Complement

100% − 2% = 98% = .98 complement

Net Amount = $326.50 × .98
$$= \$319.97$$

Markon: Cost Method—Calculating the Retail Price When the Cost and Markon Percent on Cost Are Known

When the markon is a percent of cost, the cost equals 100 percent. The retail price can be obtained by multiplying the cost by 100 percent plus the percent of markon on cost.

EXAMPLE A store purchased a jacket for $45. The dollar markup is 40% of cost. What is the retail price?

Solution
$$R = C + M$$
$$= 100\%C + 40\%C$$
$$= 140\%C$$
$$= 1.4 \times \$45$$
$$= \$63$$

Markon: Cost Method—Calculating the Cost When the Retail Price and Markon Percent on Cost Are Known

A retailer who knows how much buyers will pay for an item and knows the required markon percent necessary to make a profit must be able to determine the price to pay for that item. The cost may be found by dividing the retail price by 100 percent plus the percent of markon on cost.

EXAMPLE A merchant plans to retail jackets at $63 with a 40 percent markup on cost. What is the most the merchant can pay for the jackets to be sold at this price?

Solution

$$R = C + M$$
$$\$63 = 100\%C + 40\%C$$
$$\$63 = 140\%C$$
$$\frac{\$63}{1.40} = C$$
$$\$45 = C$$

Markon: Cost Method—Calculating the Percent of Markon on Cost When the Cost and Retail are Known

To achieve maximum profits, different markon percents may be applied to each line of merchandise. To determine the percent of markon on cost when the cost and retail are known, divide the dollar markup by the cost.

EXAMPLE A jacket cost \$45 and retails for \$63. What is the markon percent on cost?

Solution

$R = C + M$

$M = R - C$ (Subtract C from both sides.)

$M = \$63 - \$45$

$M = \$18$

$M = C \times C\%$

$C\% = M \div C$ (Divide both sides by C.)

$C\% = \$18 \div \$45$

$C\% = .4$

$C\% = 40\%$

Markon: Retail Method—Calculating the Cost When the Retail Price and Percent of Markon on Retail Are Known

The retail price equals 100 percent. Therefore, the cost can be calculated by multiplying the retail price by 100 percent and then subtracting the percent of markon on retail.

EXAMPLE A jacket that retails for $63 has a markon of 28.57 percent of retail. What is the cost of the jacket?

Solution
$$R = C + M$$
$$100\%R = C + 28.57\%R$$
$$100\%R - 28.57\%R = C$$
$$71.43\%R = C$$
$$.7143 \times \$63 = C$$
$$\$45 = C$$

Alternate Solution
$$R = C + M$$
$$\$63 = C + \$18$$
$$\$63 - 18 = C$$
$$\$45 = C$$

$(M = R \times R\%; M = \$63 \times .2857; M = \$18$

Markon: Retail Method—Calculating the Retail Price When the Cost and Percent of Markon on Retail Are Known

When the markon is a percent of retail, the retail equals 100 percent. The retail price can be calculated by dividing the cost by 100 percent less the percent of markon on retail.

EXAMPLE A jacket cost $45 and has a markon of 28.57 percent of retail. What is the retail price?

Solution

$$R = C + M$$
$$100\%R = C + 28.57\%R \qquad \text{(Subtract 28.57\% } R \text{ from both sides.)}$$
$$71.43\%R = C$$
$$R = C \div 71.43\% \qquad \text{(Divide both sides by 71.43\%.)}$$
$$R = \$45 \div .7143$$
$$R = \$63$$

Markon: Retail Method—Calculating the Percent of Markon on Retail When the Cost and Retail Are Known

The retail price equals 100 percent. The percent of markon on retail can be obtained by dividing the dollar markon by the retail price.

EXAMPLE A jacket that cost $45 retails for $63. What is the percent of markon on retail?

Solution

$R = C + M$

$M = R - C$ (Subtract C from both sides.)

$M = \$63 - \$45$

$M = \$18$

$M = R \times R\%$

$R\% = M \div R$ (Divide both sides by R.)

$R\% = \$18 \div \$63$

$R\% = .2857$

$R\% = 28.57\%$

Markdown Symbols and Formulas

Markdown Symbols

ORP = original retail price
NRP = new retail price

$m = markdown

$m = dollar markdown

%m ORP = percent of markdown on the original retail price

%m NRP = percent of markdown on the new retail price

Markdown Formulas

Dollar Amount	Percent of Original Retail Price	Percent of New Retail Price
NRP = ORP − $m	%m ORP = $m ÷ ORP	%m NRP = $m ÷ NRP
ORP = NRP + $m	NRP = ORP(100% − %m ORP)	NRP = ORP ÷ (100% + %m NRP)
$m = ORP − NRP		

Markdown—Calculating the Markdown As a Percent of the Original Retail Price

PROBLEM During a clearance sale, a merchant reduced a group of dress shirts from $10.40 to $7.80. What was the markdown as a percent of the original retail price?

Solution

$$\$m = ORP - NRP$$
$$= \$10.40 - \$7.80$$
$$= \$2.60$$
$$\%m\ ORP = \$m \div ORP$$
$$= \$2.60 \div \$10.40$$
$$= .25$$
$$= 25\%$$

Markdown—Calculating the Markdown As a Percent of the New Retail Price

PROBLEM During a clearance sale, a merchant reduced a group of dress shirts from $10.40 to $7.80. What was the markdown as a percent of the new retail price?

Solution

$$\$m = ORP - NRP$$
$$= \$10.40 - \$7.80$$
$$= \$2.60$$
$$\%m\ NRP = \$m \div NRP$$
$$= \$2.60 \div \$7.80$$
$$= .3333$$
$$= 33.33\%$$

Markdown—Calculating the New Retail Price When Markdown Is Expressed As a Percent of the Original Retail Price

PROBLEM A merchant is planning a store-wide clearance sale. All merchandise will be reduced 25 percent off the original retail price during the sale. What is the new retail price on dress shirts that were priced for $10.40?

Solution $NRP = ORP(100\% - \%m\ ORP)$
$= \$10.40 \times (100\% - 25\%)$
$= \$10.40 \times .75$
$= \$7.80$

Markdown—Calculating the New Retail Price When Markdown Is Expressed As a Percent of the New Retail Price

PROBLEM A merchant is planning a store-wide clearance sale. All merchandise will be reduced by a percent of markdown equal to 33.33 percent of the new retail price. What is the sale price on a group of dress shirts that previously sold for $10.40?

Solution
$$NRP = ORP \div (100\% + \%m\ NRP)$$
$$= \$10.40 \div (100\% + 33.33\%)$$
$$= \$10.40 \div 1.3333$$
$$= \$7.80$$

Payroll Register

Employee	Hours Worked	Rate	Weekly Salary	M/S[1]	Exemptions	Regular Pay	Overtime Pay	Gross Pay	FIT[2]	FICA[3]	HI[4]	CU[5]	Total	Net Pay
									Deductions					
Ames	42	$7.50		M	3	300.00	22.50	322.50	41.00	19.77	36.22	15	111.99	210.51
Reagan			$310	S	1	310.00	-0-	310.00	56.40	19.00	27.48		102.88	207.12
						610.00	22.50	632.50	97.40	38.77	63.70	15	214.87	417.63

1. Married/Single
2. Federal Income Tax
3. Social Security
4. Hospitalization Insurance
5. Credit Union

Learning Unit 7.1

Straight-Line Depreciation

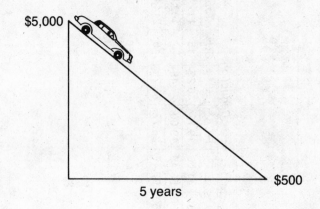

$5,000

5 years

$500

PROBLEM Find the annual depreciation for a delivery automobile that cost $5,000 with an estimated residual value of $500 and an estimated life of 5 years.

Solution *Annual depreciation* $= \dfrac{Cost - Residual\ Value}{Estimated\ Life}$

$$= \frac{\$5,000 - \$500}{5\ \text{years}}$$

$$= \frac{\$4,500}{5}$$

$$= \$900$$

PROBLEM Find the book value at the end of the second year.

Solution *Book Value = Cost − Accumulated Depreciation*
= $5,000 − $900 = $4,100
first year
= $5,000 − $1,800 = $3,200
second year

Learning Unit 7.3

Sum-of-the-Years-Digits Depreciation

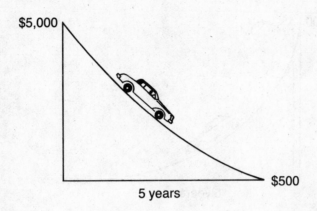

$5,000

5 years

$500

PROBLEM Find the second-year depreciation for a delivery automobile that cost $5,000 with a residual value of $500 and an estimated life of 5 years.

Solution (1) Determine the sum-of-the-years-digits.

$$S = \frac{N(N + 1)}{2}$$

$$= \frac{5(5 + 1)}{2}$$

$$= \frac{30}{2}$$

$$= 15$$

(2) Multiply the amount to be depreciated by the appropriate years-digits fraction.

Amount to be depreciated = Cost − Residual Value
$$= \$5,000 - \$500$$
$$= \$4,500$$

$$\frac{5}{15} \times \$4,500 = \$1,500 \text{ first year}$$

$$\frac{4}{15} \times \$4,500 = \$1,200 \text{ second year}$$

Declining-Balance Depreciation

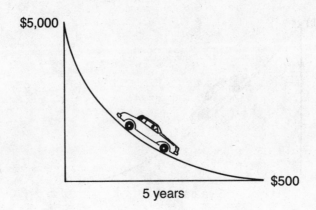

$5,000

5 years

$500

PROBLEM Find the second-year depreciation for a delivery automobile that cost $5,000 with a residual value of $500 and an estimated life of 5 years.

Solution (1) Determine the depreciation rate.

Depreciation rate = Straight-line rate × 2
= (100% ÷ 5) × 2
= 40% = .40

(2) Multiply each year's *book value* by the depreciation rate to determine the depreciation for that year.

$5,000 × .40 = $2,000 first year
$3,000 × .40 = $1,200 second year

Inventory Costing Methods: Specific Identification

Inventory Item A–36

Date	Source	Quantity	Unit Cost	Total Cost
January 1	Inventory	10 units	$17	$ 170
March 30	Purchase	10 units	19	190
July 15	Purchase	22 units	20	440
September 30	Purchase	20 units	22	440
December 1	Purchase	15 units	21	315
	Total	77 units		$1,555

PROBLEM A company had 21 units of item A–36 in the ending inventory. Based on the information in the above table, what was the cost of the ending inventory of this item? One unit was from the beginning inventory; 2 units were purchased March 30; 6 units were purchased September 30; and, 12 units were purchased December 1.

Solution

January 1	Inventory	1 unit	@ $17 =	$ 17
March 30	Purchase	2 units	@ $19 =	$ 38
September 30	Purchase	6 units	@ $22 =	$132
December 1	Purchase	12 units	@ $21 =	$252
			Total cost =	$439

Learning Unit 8.1

Inventory Costing Methods: First-In, First-Out (FIFO)

Inventory Item A–36

Date	Source	Quantity	Unit Cost	Total Cost
January 1	Inventory	10 units	$17	$ 170
March 30	Purchase	10 units	19	190
July 15	Purchase	22 units	20	440
September 30	Purchase	20 units	22	440
December 1	Purchase	15 units	21	315
	Total	77 units		$1,555

PROBLEM A company had 21 units of item A–36 in the ending inventory. Based on the information in the above table, what was the cost of the ending inventory of this item if the company uses FIFO to determine the cost of the inventory?

Solution December 1   15 units @ $21 = $315
September 30 6 units @ $22 = $132
Total cost = $447

Inventory Costing Methods: Last-In, First-Out (LIFO)

Inventory Item A–36

Date	Source	Quantity	Unit Cost	Total Cost
January 1	Inventory	10 units	$17	$ 170
March 30	Purchase	10 units	19	190
July 15	Purchase	22 units	20	440
September 30	Purchase	20 units	22	440
December 1	Purchase	15 units	21	315
	Total	77 units		$1,555

PROBLEM A company had 21 units of item A–36 in the ending inventory. Based on the information in the above table, what was the cost of the ending inventory of this item if the company uses LIFO to determine the cost of the inventory?

Solution

January 1	10 units	@ $17 =	$170
March 30	10 units	@ $19 =	$190
July 15	1 unit	@ $20 =	$ 20
		Total cost =	$380

Inventory Costing Methods: Average Cost

Inventory Item A–36

Date	Source	Quantity	Unit Cost	Total Cost
January 1	Inventory	10 units	$17	$ 170
March 30	Purchase	10 units	19	190
July 15	Purchase	22 units	20	440
September 30	Purchase	20 units	22	440
December 1	Purchase	15 units	21	315
	Total	77 units		$1,555

PROBLEM A company had 21 units of item A–36 in the ending inventory. Based on the information in the above table, what was the cost of the ending inventory of this item if the company uses the average cost method to determine the cost of the inventory?

Solution *Average unit cost* $= \dfrac{\textit{Total cost of all units}}{\textit{Total number of units available}}$

$$= \frac{\$1,555}{77}$$

$$= \$20.19$$

Cost of the 21 units $= \$20.19 \times 21$
$$= \$423.99$$

Cost of Merchandise Sold

PROBLEM Determine the cost of merchandise sold based upon the following inventories and net purchases.

Merchandise inventory, January 1	$ 4,500
Merchandise inventory, December 31	6,000
Net purchases for the year	130,000

Solution

Merchandise inventory, January 1	$ 4,500
Net purchases	130,000
Merchandise available for sale	$134,500
Less merchandise inventory, December 31	6,000
Cost of merchandise sold	$128,500

Central Supply Company
Comparative Income Statement with Vertical Analysis
Years Ended December 31, 19_1, and December 31, 19_2

	19_2	Percent	19_1	Percent
Revenue:				
Net sales	$188,150	100.00	$167,340	100.00
Operating expenses:				
Cost of merchandise sold	82,800	44.00	77,210	46.14
Salaries expense	33,600	17.86	31,200	18.64
Wages expense	29,200	15.52	27,800	16.61
Depreciation expense	5,400	2.87	5,100	3.05
Advertising expense	4,000	2.13	4,000	2.39
Utilities expense	3,400	1.81	2,830	1.69
Supplies used	1,600	.85	1,600	.96
Miscellaneous expense	1,200	.64	1,420	.85
Total expenses	$161,200	85.68	$151,160	90.33
Net income	$ 26,950	14.32	$ 16,180	9.67

Central Supply Company
Comparative Balance Sheet with Vertical Analysis
December 31, 19_1, and December 31, 19_2

	19_2	Percent	19_1	Percent
Assets				
Current assets:				
Cash	$ 5,000	3.48	$ 3,500	2.52
Accounts receivable	18,000	12.53	17,200	12.37
Supplies	700	.49	850	.61
Merchandise inventory	40,000	27.84	32,100	23.09
Total current assets	$ 63,700	44.33	$ 53,650	38.58
Plant assets:				
Equipment	$ 40,000	27.84	$ 40,000	28.77
Less accumulated depreciation	15,000	10.44	11,600	8.34
	$ 25,000	17.40	$ 28,400	20.42
Building	$ 50,000	34.79	$ 50,000	35.96
Less accumulated depreciation	10,000	6.96	8,000	5.75
	$ 40,000	27.84	$ 42,000	30.20
Land	$ 15,000	10.44	$ 15,000	10.79
Total plant assets	$ 80,000	55.68	$ 85,400	61.42
Total assets	$143,700	100.00	$139,050	100.00
Liabilities				
Current Liabilities:				
Accounts payable	$ 20,000	13.92	$ 18,500	13.30
Notes payable	13,000	9.05	14,200	10.21
Total current liabilities	$ 33,000	22.96	$ 32,700	23.52
Long-term liabilities:				
Mortgage payable	$ 29,500	20.53	$ 30,200	21.72
Total liabilities	$ 62,500	43.49	$ 62,900	45.24
Capital				
Sam Sims, capital	$ 81,200	56.51	$ 76,150	54.76
Total liabilities and capital	$143,700	100.00	$139,050	100.00

Learning Unit 9.1

Central Supply Company
Comparative Income Statement with Horizontal Analysis
Years Ended December 31, 19_1, and December 31, 19_2

	Year Ended December 31		Amount of Increase or (Decrease)	Percent of Increase or (Decrease)
	19_2	19_1		
Revenue:				
Net sales	$188,150	$167,340	$20,810	12.44
Operating expenses:				
Cost of merchandise sold	82,800	77,210	5,590	7.24
Salaries expense	33,600	31,200	2,400	7.69
Wages expense	29,200	27,800	1,400	5.04
Depreciation expense	5,400	5,100	300	5.88
Advertising expense	4,000	4,000		
Utilities expense	3,400	2,830	570	20.14
Supplies used	1,600	1,600		
Miscellaneous expense	1,200	1,420	(220)	(15.49)
Total expenses	$161,200	$151,160	$10,040	6.64
Net income	$ 26,950	$ 16,180	$10,770	66.56

Central Supply Company
Comparative Balance Sheet with Horizontal Analysis
December 31, 19_1, and December 31, 19_2

	Year Ended December 31		Amount of Increase or (Decrease)	Percent of Increase or (Decrease)
	19_2	19_1		
Assets				
Current assets:				
Cash	$ 5,000	$ 3,500	$ 1,500	42.86
Accounts receivable	18,000	17,200	800	4.65
Supplies	700	850	(150)	(17.65)
Merchandise inventory	40,000	32,100	7,900	24.61
Total current assets	$ 63,700	$ 53,650	$10,050	18.73
Plant assets:				
Equipment	$ 40,000	$ 40,000		
Less accumulated depreciation	$ 15,000	11,600	$ 3,400	29.31
	$ 25,000	$ 28,400	$ (3,400)	(11.97)
Building	$ 50,000	$ 50,000		
Less accumulated depreciation	10,000	8,000	$ 2,000	25.00
	$ 40,000	$ 42,000	$ (2,000)	(4.76)
Land	$ 15,000	$15,000		
Total plant assets	$ 80,000	$ 85,400	$ (5,400)	(6.32)
Total assets	$143,700	$139,050	$ 4,650	3.34
Liabilities				
Current liabilities:				
Accounts payable	$ 20,000	$ 18,500	$ 1,500	8.11
Notes payable	13,000	14,200	(1,200)	(8.45)
Total current liabilities	$ 33,000	$ 32,700	$ 300	.92
Long-term liabilities:				
Mortgage payable	$ 29,500	$ 30,200	$ (700)	(2.32)
Total liabilities	$ 62,500	$ 62,900	$ (400)	(.64)
Capital				
Sam Sims, capital	$ 81,200	$ 76,150	$ 5,050	6.63
Total liabilities and capital	$143,700	$139,050	$ 4,650	3.34

Financial Ratios: Current Ratio

PROBLEM On December 31, Yeager's Sporting Goods had $80,000 in current assets and $40,000 in current liabilities. What was the company's current ratio?

Solution $Current\ ratio = \dfrac{Current\ assets}{Current\ liabilities}$

$$= \frac{\$80,000}{\$40,000}$$

$$= \frac{2}{1}\ \text{or}\ 2\!:\!1$$

Financial Ratios: Acid Test Ratio

PROBLEM On December 31, Yeager's Sporting Goods had $50,000 in quick assets and $40,000 in current liabilities. What was the company's acid test ratio?

Solution $Acid\ test\ ratio = \dfrac{Quick\ assets}{Current\ liabilities}$

$$= \dfrac{\$50,000}{\$40,000}$$

$$= \dfrac{1.25}{1} \text{ or } 1.25:1$$

Learning Unit 9.2

Financial Ratios: Ratio of Plant Assets to Long-Term Liabilities

PROBLEM On December 31, Yeager's Sporting Goods had $100,000 in plant assets and $40,000 in long-term liabilities. What was the company's ratio of plant assets to long-term liabilities?

Solution Ratio of plant assets to long-term liabilities

$$= \frac{\$100,000}{\$\ 40,000}$$

$$= \frac{2.5}{1} \text{ or } 2.5:1$$

Financial Ratios: Rate of Return on Total Assets

PROBLEM Yeager's Sporting Goods had total assets of $180,000 on January 1 and $187,000 on December 31. Net income for the year was $20,000. What was the company's rate of return on total assets?

Solution Total assets $= \dfrac{\$180,000 + \$187,000}{2}$

$= \$183,500$

Rate of return on total assets

$= \dfrac{\$\ 20,000}{\$183,500}$

$= .109 = 10.9\%$

Financial Ratios: Rate of Return on Owner's Equity

PROBLEM Yeager's Sporting Goods had capital of $100,000 at the end of the year. Net income for the year was $20,000. What was the rate of return on owner's equity?

Solution Rate of return on owner's equity

$$= \frac{\$\ 20,000}{\$100,000}$$

$$= .2 = 20\%$$

Learning Unit 9.2

Inventory Turnover

PROBLEM Yeager's Sporting Goods had merchandise inventory of $30,000 on January 1 and $34,000 on December 31. The cost of merchandise sold for the year was $64,000. What was the inventory turnover?

Solution $Inventory\ turnover = \dfrac{Cost\ of\ merchandise\ sold}{Average\ inventory}$

$\text{Average inventory} = \dfrac{\$30{,}000 + \$34{,}000}{2}$

$= \$32{,}000$

$\text{Inventory turnover} = \dfrac{\$64{,}000}{\$32{,}000}$

$= 2$

Branch Supply Incorporated
Bank Reconciliation Statement
June 30, 19_1

Balance per bank statement			$1,348.83	
Add: Deposit of June 30 (deposit in transit)			2,800.00	
			$4,148.83	
Deduct: Outstanding checks				
Check #102	$ 76.40			
Check #104	620.71		697.11	
Adjusted balance per bank statement			$3,451.72	

Balance per company records			$2,056.22	
Add: Note collected by the bank			1,500.00	
			$3,556.22	
Deduct: Collection fee	$ 3.00			
Service charge	1.50			
Draft	100.00		104.50	
Adjusted balance per company records			$3,451.72	

Promissory Note (Interest Bearing)

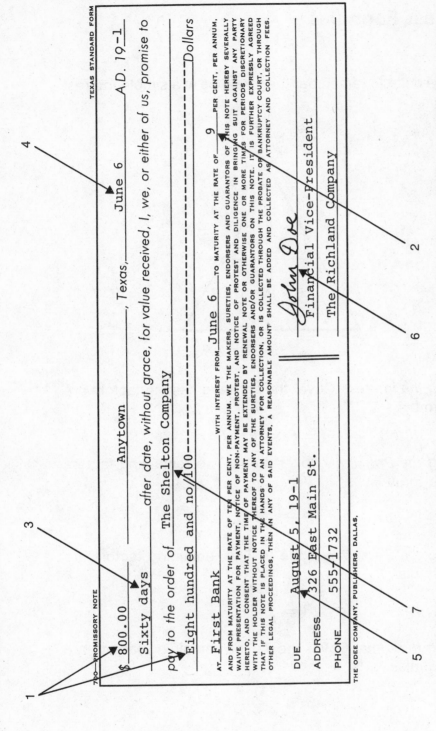

TEXAS STANDARD FORM

700— PROMISSORY NOTE

$ 800.00   Anytown   , Texas,   June 6   A.D. 19–1

Sixty days   after date, without grace, for value received, I, we, or either of us, promise to

pay to the order of   The Shelton Company

Eight hundred and no/100------------------------------------Dollars

AT First Bank   WITH INTEREST FROM June 6   TO MATURITY AT THE RATE OF   9   PER CENT. PER ANNUM, AND FROM MATURITY AT THE RATE OF TEN PER CENT. PER ANNUM. WE THE MAKERS, SURETIES, ENDORSERS AND GUARANTORS OF THIS NOTE HEREBY SEVERALLY WAIVE PRESENTATION FOR PAYMENT, NOTICE OF NON-PAYMENT, PROTEST, AND NOTICE OF PROTEST AND DILIGENCE IN BRINGING SUIT AGAINST ANY PARTY HERETO, AND CONSENT THAT THE TIME OF PAYMENT MAY BE EXTENDED BY RENEWAL NOTE OR OTHERWISE ONE OR MORE TIMES FOR PERIODS DISCRETIONARY WITH THE HOLDER WITHOUT NOTICE THEREOF TO ANY OF THE SURETIES, ENDORSERS AND/OR GUARANTORS ON THIS NOTE. IT IS FURTHER EXPRESSLY AGREED THAT IF THIS NOTE IS PLACED IN THE HANDS OF AN ATTORNEY FOR COLLECTION, OR IS COLLECTED THROUGH THE PROBATE OR BANKRUPTCY COURT, OR THROUGH OTHER LEGAL PROCEEDINGS, THEN IN ANY OF SAID EVENTS, A REASONABLE AMOUNT SHALL BE ADDED AND COLLECTED AS ATTORNEY AND COLLECTION FEES.

John Doe

Financial Vice-President

The Richland Company

DUE   August 5, 19–1

ADDRESS   326 East Main St.

PHONE   555-1732

THE ODEE COMPANY, PUBLISHERS, DALLAS.

1. The *principal* ($800.00) is the amount of the debt. It is the amount of money borrowed in the credit transaction.

2. The *rate* (9 percent) expresses the value paid for use of the borrowed money. It is usually stated in annual, or yearly, terms.

3. The *time* (60 days) is the period for which the money is borrowed.

4. The *date* (June 6) is the date the note was issued.

5. The *maturity date* (August 5) is the day the principal and interest are due. It is often called the due date.

6. The *maker* (The Richland Company) is the individual or company issuing the note and borrowing the money.

7. The *payee* (The Shelton Company) is the individual or company extending the credit.

Interest Formulas

Use the delta to remember the formulas in a simple-interest problem.

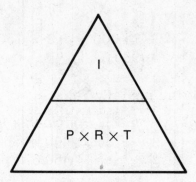

Finding the Interest. Cover the *I*. The remaining factors are the formula.

$$I = P \times R \times T$$

Finding the Principal. Cover the *P*. The remaining factors are the formula.

$$P = \frac{I}{R \times T}$$

Finding the Rate. Cover the *R*. The remaining factors are the formula.

$$R = \frac{I}{P \times T}$$

Finding the Time. Cover the *T*. The remaining factors are the formula.

$$T = \frac{I}{P \times R}$$

Remember to multiply your answer by 360.

Simple Interest

PROBLEM Find the interest on $1,400 at 12% for 130 days.

Solution *Interest = Principal × Rate × Time*

$$= \$1,400 \times .12 \times \frac{130}{360}$$

$$= \$1,400 \times .12 \times 130 \div 360$$

$$= \$60.67$$

PROBLEM Find the maturity value.

Solution *Maturity value = Principal + Interest*

$$= \$1,400 + \$60.67$$

$$= \$1,460.67$$

Finding the Principal

PROBLEM The interest on a 12 percent, 130-day loan is $60.67. What is the principal?

Solution $P = \dfrac{I}{R \times T}$

$$= 60.67 \div \left(.12 \times \frac{130}{360}\right)$$

$$= \frac{60.67}{.04333333}$$

$$= \$1{,}400$$

Finding the Rate

PROBLEM $1,400 is invested for 130 days and earns $60.67 interest. What is the rate of interest?

Solution $R = \dfrac{I}{P \times T}$

$$= 60.67 \div \left(1{,}400 \times \frac{130}{360}\right)$$

$$= \frac{60.67}{505.55555}$$

$$= .12 = 12\%$$

Finding the Time

PROBLEM How long will it take $1,400 at 12 percent to earn $60.67 in interest?

Solution
$$T = \frac{I}{P \times R}$$
$$= \frac{60.67}{1,400 \times .12}$$
$$= \frac{60.67}{168}$$
$$= .3611309 \times 360$$
$$= 130 \text{ days}$$

Bank Discount

PROBLEM Find the bank discount and net proceeds for a note with a maturity value of $1,460.67. The bank charges 13 percent and will hold the note for 120 days.

Solution (a) *Bank discount = Maturity value × Discount rate × Discount period*
= $1,460.67 × .13 × 120 ÷ 360
= $63.30

(b) *Net proceeds = Maturity value − Bank Discount*
= $1,460.67 − $63.30
= $1,397.37

Metric Measurement Conversion Table

10^3	10^2	10^1	10^0	10^{-1}	10^{-2}	10^{-3}
kilo-	hecto-	deka-	GRAM METER LITER	deci-	centi-	milli-
1 000	100	10	1	0.1	0.01	0.001

Beginning Numbers in the Decimal and Binary Systems

Decimal Number	Binary Number	Binary Positional Interpretation
0	0	0 ones
1	1	1 one
2	10	1 two + 0 ones
3	11	1 two + 1 one
4	100	1 four + 0 twos + 0 ones
5	101	1 four + 0 twos + 1 one
6	110	1 four + 1 two + 0 ones
7	111	1 four + 1 two + 1 one
8	1000	1 eight + 0 fours + 0 twos + 0 ones
9	1001	1 eight + 0 fours + 0 twos + 1 one
10	1010	1 eight + 0 fours + 1 two + 0 ones

Changing Binary Numbers to Decimal Numbers

To change a binary number to a decimal number, multiply
each digit by its place value and add the results.

EXAMPLE Change the binary number 101001 to a decimal
number.

Solution

Binary number	1	0	1	0	0	1
Multiply	×	×	×	×	×	×
Place values	32	16	8	4	2	1

Add the results $32 + 0 + 8 + 0 + 0 + 1 = 41$

Changing Decimal Numbers to Binary Numbers

To change a decimal number to a binary number, divide
repeatedly by 2. The remainders are the required binary
digits. Check your answer by changing the binary number
back to a decimal number.

EXAMPLE Change 22 to a binary number.

Solution $22 \div 2 = 11$, remainder 0
$11 \div 2 = 5$, remainder 1
$5 \div 2 = 2$, remainder 1
$2 \div 2 = 1$, remainder 0
$1 \div 2 = 0$, remainder 1

10110   binary number

Check Binary number   1   0   1   1   0
Multiply   ×   ×   ×   ×   ×
Place values   16   8   4   2   1
Add the results $16 + 0 + 4 + 2 + 0 = 22$ decimal number